# Reforming
## Intelligence Agencies
### Pakistan's Transitional Democracy

# Attention Authors

Manas Publications is fighting a war to tell the world that India can win the battle not only by the bullet but also by pen. We are converting fighters into writers. There is no dearth of intellectuals in our country, however, their knowledge is confined to them only. No sincere effort has been made by any other publisher to channelise their knowledge, which is why the talent of every intellectual remains latent. An author always presents the raw material in the shape of a manuscript and it is the job of the publisher to convert it to a finished product. Manas has been continually motivating intellectuals and publishing their manuscripts for more than two decades and would like to publish your manuscript too. If you or your colleagues have a manuscript ready for publication or are working on it, contact us with a detailed synopsis and list of contents. Manas will also suggest you a suitable title for writing related to your area of expertise. Manas is known for its publishing quality. We take utmost care in publishing and also give wide publicity to the book and its author through our national and international distribution network.

# Reforming
## Intelligence Agencies
### Pakistan's Transitional Democracy

Frederic Grare

**Manas Publications**
**(We Convert Fighters into Writers)**
New Delhi-110002 (INDIA)

# MANAS PUBLICATIONS

(Publishers, Library Suppliers, Importers & Exporters)
4402/5-A, Ansari Road (Opp. HDFC Bank)
Darya Ganj, New Delhi-110 002 (INDIA)
Off. © 23260783, 23265523, Res. © 23842660
Fax: 011-23272766
E-mail:    manaspublications@vsnl.com
            manaspublications@gmail.com
Website:  www.manaspublications.in

ISBN 978-81-7049-398-3
Rs.595

Reprinted with the permission of the publisher, Carnegie Endowment for International Peace, Washington.

*Typeset at*
**Manas Publications**

*Printed in India at*
RK Print Services, Delhi
and published by Mrs Suman Lata for
**Manas Publications**, 4402/5-A, Ansari Road
(Opp. HDFC Bank),
Darya Ganj, New Delhi-110 002 (INDIA)

# Contents

# ACKNOWLEDGEMENTS

This report would not have been possible without the help of many people. I would like to thank in particular in Chile: Congresswoman Carolina Toha, Congressman Jorge Burgos, General Emilio Cheyre, Mr. Gustavo Villalobo, head of Chile's National Intelligence Agency, Mr. Gustavo Fouilloux, former head of the Department for Public Security and Intelligence, and Ms. Javiera Blanco, Deputy Director of Police. Many thanks also to Marina Spindler, who helped identify contacts in Chile, and to Ishaias Sharon, who assisted with translation. In Indonesia, my gratitude goes to many, in particular, Mr. William Tuchrello from the Library of Congress, Mr. H. S. Dillon, Ambassador Gelbard, and many others. The report has also benefited from the advice of many whom I will not name in Pakistan. I am also grateful to Carnegie, where I spent three wonderful years, and to my accomplices there, Ashley Tellis and George Perkovich. Special thanks also to Ilonka Oszvald, David Donadio, and Mary Marik, who made the report readable, and to Vicki O'Reilly, who managed to make the few administrative duties associated with the conduct of the report almost a pleasure. The responsibility for the ideas and opinions expressed in the present document is, of course, entirely mine.

# SUMMARY

The purpose of the present report is to analyze the intelligence agencies' role in Pakistan's political life through a better understanding of the agencies' objectives and mechanisms. Because Pakistan's civilian governments have been victims of the agencies' manipulation in the past, the new and very fragile government cannot ignore the decisive role of the intelligence agencies in Pakistani politics if it wants to counter the direct and more subtle manifestations of military control. The domestic political role of intelligence agencies is always a combination of three elements: militarization, comprehensive political surveillance, and state terror. The intensity and relative importance of each component varies over time and according to the specific situations in each country, but all three are always present. Terror as it applies to individuals or groups can be carried out by proxies and is intermittent, but it remains an essential element of the system. An intelligence agency's reputation for ruthlessness is often as important as its actual efficiency.

The reform of the intelligence agencies is therefore imperative, and the depoliticization of the intelligence process is as much an element of national reconciliation as of consolidation of power. To achieve its objectives, this report draws on interviews conducted in Pakistan as well as on related literature. It also examines similar attempts at reasserting civilian control over intelligence agencies in two democratizing military dictatorships, Indonesia and Chile. In all three countries, intelligence agencies were— and in the case of Pakistan still are— trying to achieve a similar set of objectives regarding social control, the need to protect the regime against all sources of disturbance, and promoting the passive acceptance of regime policies by the population. Neither Indonesia nor Chile has been completely successful in bringing its intelligence agencies under democratic control but both were forced to reform their intelligence services and simultaneously reduce the scope of military autonomy vis-à-vis elected officials. This is what Pakistan will have to do in order to consolidate its nascent democracy.

# 1

# THE

# ISSUE

Full-blown military regimes have become a dying breed. In Asia alone, the role of the military in politics has declined considerably since the 1980s. By 2000, only two regimes in the region were controlled by the military: Burma and Pakistan. As of 2008, this number is unchanged, but it could be argued that Bangladesh has taken Pakistan's place. Since the February 18, 2008 elections in Pakistan, in which General Pervez Musharraf (retired) and his cronies were spectacularly rejected, civilians are back to power in Islamabad.

Yet, Pakistan can at best be qualified as a transitional democracy, and its future remains uncertain. The civilians have conquered a political space that until now has been nonexistent, but they do not fully control the state apparatus. Their victory was an expression of popular aspirations to democracy after eight years of military dictatorship. The civilian victory was only possible, however, because the new chief of army staff (COAS), General Ashfaq Parvez Kayani, made a deliberate decision to remain neutral in the election, in effect distancing himself from his predecessor. Despite this progress, there has been little structural change in civil-military relations. The army remains the dominant actor in Pakistan's political life.

Given the leading role of the military in Pakistani politics, the reform of Pakistan's intelligence agencies constitutes a central issue. The role of the intelligence agencies has always been highly controversial. They have too often been used to meddle in the country's domestic politics. Pakistan's military governments, like those of Generals Ayub Khan, Yahya Khan, Zia-ul-Haq, and Pervez Musharraf, and civilian governments like that of Zulfikar Ali Bhutto have all used the intelligence agencies extensively for political purposes. Civilian and military regimes differ, however, in the degree of control they are able to exercise over the intelligence agencies, which tend to consider the military their natural patron.

"Operations against dissenting politicians, objective intellectuals and other activists were carried out through systematic harassment, disinformation campaigns, fictitious trials, kidnappings, torture and assassination," wrote Iftikhar H. Malik.[1] Intelligence agencies have also been systematically used for political engineering. Military agencies such as Military Intelligence (MI) and the Inter-Services

Intelligence (ISI) have gone far beyond their professional domains to conduct surveillance on civilians and political opponents of the military regime as well as masterminding alliances of co-opted civilians, occasionally playing on religious and ethnic sentiments and more generally along all faultlines in an already divided Pakistani society. For that matter, military agencies have sometimes employed means they should have used to combat terrorism against Pakistani citizens.

The role of the intelligence agencies, and of the ISI in particular, may occasionally have been exaggerated. From time to time, the agencies have made easy scapegoats for politicians eager to justify their political misfortunes through conspiracy theories. Intelligence agencies have nevertheless played a central role in a number of political developments in the country and have been a favorite instrument of control during past regimes. Their reform therefore shapes the survival of the new regime to a large extent and, as stated by Hassan Abbas, "desperately needs the attention of the new government before it succumbs to a series of clandestine operations."[2]

Because Pakistan's civilian governments have been victims of the agencies' manipulation in the past, the new and very fragile government cannot ignore the decisive role of the intelligence agencies in Pakistani politics if it wants to counter the direct and more subtle manifestations of military control. The reform of the intelligence agencies is therefore imperative, and the depoliticization of the intelligence process is as much an element of national reconciliation as of consolidation of power.

## OBJECTIVES OF THIS ANALYSIS

This report is a continuation of previous work by the Carnegie Endowment for International Peace on redefining Western strategies toward Pakistan, and it is based on the premise that controlling the intelligence agencies is only one specific aspect of the larger democratization issue.

The purpose of this paper is not to indulge in any conspiracy theory, nor to hold the intelligence agencies responsible for every domestic evil Pakistan faces, but to analyze the agencies' role in Pakistan's political life. Through a better understanding of the agencies' objectives and mechanisms, we can rectify the distorted perceptions surrounding them. The report also touches on the consequences of the agencies' domestic security operations and, to some extent, Pakistan's social and national unity, and it examines past attempts at controlling the agencies. This report therefore has both analytical and normative dimensions.

The literature on the Pakistani intelligence agencies is scarce and is often of poor quality. Most of it focuses on the regional role of the ISI and its support for radical Islamic groups, ignoring the fact that this support constitutes an important aspect of the process of political control. Even the ISI's manipulation of Islamic radical groups is not limited to foreign policy objectives; it is also used in a domestic context.

The prevailing literature also tends to paint a distorted picture of the political machinations of the intelligence agencies. The quasi-exclusive focus on radical Islamic groups hides a larger reality in which ostensibly secular organizations such as the Muttahida

Qaumi Movement (MQM), a mohajir[3] political party, are important actors in the manipulation of the political process, although they are themselves at times victims of such manipulations. This distortion in "favor" of the radical Islamic groups, and the subsequent absence of other (and often more effective) forms of manipulation, contributes—deliberately or not—to the manipulation itself. Intelligence agencies, for example, spread the idea of an Islamist threat in a potentially extremist society, which made the presence of a military regime in power a security imperative.

In its normative dimension, this report tries to answer questions related not to the technicalities of intelligence and covert operations, but to the constitutional, legal, and political ways by which they could be made accountable. It also draws from experiences elsewhere in the world to make recommendations for Pakistan.

## BARRIERS TO REFORM THE INTELLIGENCE AGENCIES IN PAKISTAN

Reforming the intelligence agencies is not exclusively a legal and constitutional issue, however. During the 1990s, the military never directly opposed the nomination of directors general of the ISI even if it did not approve them, so, strictly speaking, it never broke the law. It did, however, bypass the democratic process, ostracizing the government's nominees and ensuring that their leadership remained ineffective.

Nor is reform purely a matter of organizational restructuring. Reform should start with "clarifying the philosophy, and redefining the mission, focus and priorities of intelligence in order to establish a new culture of intelligence."[4] Reforming the intelligence agencies therefore requires not only a change in the state, but a change of the state of mind of the actors involved. It must be understood in the larger context of civil-military relations. In Pakistan's case, this will require building trust, which will be particularly difficult not only because of past relationships between civilians and the military but also because it presents a structural contradiction: the lack of trust is precisely why the agencies need to be controlled.

As a consequence, redefining the role of the intelligence agencies inevitably has far-reaching political implications. Intelligence agencies are always primarily an expression of the fundamental character of the state. In the specific case of Pakistan, the agencies' activities reflect the traditional dominance of the army, which has translated into standard operating procedures such as intimidation of individuals and groups, bribery, manipulation, occasional murder, and political surveillance of virtually the entire population, articulated with a need for legitimacy and support from the United States and other powers. Reasserting civilian control is therefore both the condition and the consequence of a true and lasting democratization process.

Reforming the intelligence agencies to make them accountable to civilian governments is indeed complex. Overall, "the objective is that . . . intelligence agencies should be insulated from political abuse without being isolated from executive power."[5] But several categories of difficulties can be identified at this stage:

*Institutional.* As asserted by Gregory Weeks, "Intelligence reform is difficult because it involves the co-ordination of multiple intelligence agencies, specification of authority between the military and the executive, legislative and judicial branches, restructuring, all within the context of promoting national security while assuring human rights."[6]

*Lack of an intelligence culture.* Linked to the previous problem is the new government's lack of knowledge of intelligence culture. The reform of the intelligence agencies in Pakistan will inevitably face a dilemma: it will require a level of expertise that cannot be improvised and will most likely be found only within the ranks of the military, since military officers have so far been the only ones in charge. The problem may be resolved temporarily by recruiting officers sympathetic to the civilian government, but it does not eliminate the possibility of conflicting loyalties and unbalanced expertise.

*Timing.* Timing is always an issue for any reform because reform always implies a measure of disruption of existing mechanisms and institutions. In this case, timing is an even more acute challenge because the desired democratic transition is sought in a context where political violence and armed conflicts are growing.

Indeed, terrorism has not disappeared in the wake of the national and provincial assembly elections. Any disruption of the existing intelligence agencies is seen as likely to impede the ever-urgent need to fight terrorism, before which even democracy is too often considered secondary.

This consideration reflects both reality and, to an extent, a false problem. The question of democratic control of the intelligence agencies is a matter of accountability and orientation, not professional skill.

The direction of these organizations has had much less to do with their official primary concerns than with the domestic interests of the ruling elite, in which case reform is imperative. It is essential to ensure, for example, that terrorism is no longer the result of the traditional manipulation of extremist groups by the intelligence agencies for domestic and foreign policy purposes. It should be acknowledged, however, that terrorism is sometimes the paradoxical result of the agencies' attempts to reassert control—as after the military intervention in Islamabad's Red Mosque to dislodge the extremists who had sought shelter there— thus making an in-depth reform of the agencies more difficult.

*Political consolidation versus counterterrorism.* Intelligence reforms take place in a context where reform depends on the strength of a political body whose weakening is a top priority of the military.

This context creates conflicting priorities for the new government: political consolidation, on the one hand, versus counterterrorism on the other. Uncertainty regarding the military's actual position on counterterrorism is an additional difficulty. Disorder (or its appearance) can serve political and military elites alike: the former because it delegitimizes any opposition, the latter because it demonstrates their indispensability. For the same reasons, it is not clear whether the international community will facilitate or frustrate political consolidation in Pakistan. For foreign governments, the temptation will be strong to cooperate directly with the intelligence agencies, thus legitimizing them, at the expense of the Pakistan government's control over them. This difficulty could, however, be turned into an advantage: because intelligence officials do not have to fear for their jobs, it could be easier for leaders to make them accept the necessary changes.

But the security context is not the only obstacle to better control of the intelligence agencies. The relationship of the intelligence agencies to democracy is almost always uneasy owing to the nature of their activities.

One explanation is the lack of transparency regarding the objectives of the agencies; but the situation is further complicated by the restriction of information about any given operation to a small number of officials, the lack of formal procedures for an operation's approval, and the lack of records on the agencies' activities, among other things. The means of controlling the agencies' activities are almost always indirect, such as the approval of budgets, political responsibility for nominations of intelligence officials to key executive positions, and, in some countries, a posteriori control of some operations. Although no intelligence agency operates outside a minimal legal framework, the Pakistan armed forces, and consequently the intelligence agencies, retain a high level of autonomy.

Ultimately, reforming the intelligence services will result only from changes within them to accommodate the new democratic situation. According to Gregory Weeks, "Efforts should aim at strict compliance with the constitutional order and specific legislation over the intelligence agencies,"[7] but given the nature of the agencies' activities, the means to enforce this compliance will have to be found in the vigilance of society as a whole as much as in the legal framework designed to control them.

# 2

# A
# COMPARATIVE
# ══════════APPROACH

To achieve its objectives, this report draws on interviews conducted in Pakistan as well as on related literature. It also examines similar attempts at reasserting civilian control over intelligence agencies in two democratizing military dictatorships, Indonesia and Chile.

The fourth-most-populous country in the world and the largest with a majority Muslim population, Indonesia shares many characteristics with Pakistan. Straddling critical straits and sea lanes, it is geostrategically no less important than the "land of the pure," with which it shares serious concerns about ethnic and religious conflicts. Like Pakistan, it also became a major battlefield in the war on terrorism after September 11, 2001. During the entire Suharto dictatorship, "the key apparatus in all of this was the large and well funded network of military and nominally civilian intelligence organizations that make up the Indonesian state."[8] Terrorist groups there are no longer seen as local threats but as part of larger and more dangerous global networks.[9] The Indonesian military, which had been part of the country's political leadership for more than thirty years, coincidentally was dislodged from power at about the same time the military was taking the helm of political power in Pakistan.[10]

In Chile, too, the repressive role of the intelligence agencies was the result of the emergence of a dictatorship. The National Intelligence Directorate (DINA) was formed in the immediate aftermath of the 1973 coup d'état, ostensibly as a mechanism to coordinate the intelligence services of the three branches of the military (army, navy, and air force) but effectively as a secret police force to repress dissidents within the state. DINA was succeeded in 1977 by the National Information Center, which was also later dismantled after the country returned to civilian rule in 1990.

In all three countries—Indonesia, Chile, and Pakistan—intelligence establishments and the role of the militaries within them became infamous. Although the abuses of human rights and civil liberties have been well publicized in the cases of Indonesia and Chile, they remain largely unknown in Pakistan, where the focus has been on the relationship between the intelligence agencies at home and Islamic terrorism abroad. The perception of these institutions as a domestic problem is a more recent phenomenon, linked to the emergence of a violent Taliban movement in Pakistan itself; but the Pakistani Taliban are still seen as a continuity of ISI interference rather than an issue in themselves.

In all three countries, intelligence agencies were—and in the case of Pakistan still are—trying to achieve a similar set of objectives regarding social control, the need to protect the regime against all sources of disturbance, and promoting the passive acceptance of regime policies by the population.

The domestic political role of intelligence agencies is a combination of three elements: militarization, comprehensive political surveillance, and state terror. The intensity and relative importance of each component varies over time and according to the specific situations in each country, but all three are always present. Terror as it applies to individuals or groups can be carried out by proxies and is intermittent, but it remains an essential element of the system. An intelligence agency's reputation for ruthlessness is often as important as its actual efficiency.

Indonesia and Chile are appropriate case studies because both were forced to reform their intelligence services and simultaneously reduce the scope of military autonomy vis-à-vis elected officials. This is what Pakistan will have to do in order to consolidate its nascent democracy.

Neither Indonesia nor Chile has been completely successful in bringing its intelligence agencies under democratic control. Both countries are at different stages of the process, but both have seen significant improvements in their respective situations. The choice of these two countries as case studies reflects a willingness to seek out practical objectives rather than search for some unattainable ideal. It remains to be seen whether the role of the intelligence agencies in these two countries has been reoriented as significantly as could have been expected. Yet even the limitations and eventual failures of intelligence reorganization in Indonesia and Chile yield valuable information. The processes, as much as the results, by which these two countries are reasserting civilian control over their intelligence agencies constitute an important part of the present report.

The choice of countries examined also results from a deliberate attempt to minimize so-called culturalist considerations, and religious biases in particular, in the occasional comparisons with Pakistan. Indonesia's status as a Muslim country confronted by Islamic radicalism and separatist tendencies did not prevent the democratization process from taking place there. By contrast, being predominantely Christian neither stopped Chile from becoming a military dictatorship nor prevented its return to democracy. Factors other than religion obviously played a role in both processes, and it is thus essential to eliminate religion as a defining factor when one addresses democratization in a Muslim country.

Ultimately, it should be emphasized that this report purports to be no more than a preliminary study. It is based on open sources and interviews, and the information it contains is admittedly incomplete. Although the ISI has been implicated in violence throughout the hot spots of the Indian subcontinent and Afghanistan and its activities have generated a vast literature, the political role of the Pakistani intelligence agencies, and the ISI in particular, has had very little written about it although it is widely discussed in Pakistan. For obvious reasons, both the actors and the victims— and they are sometimes the same—are reluctant to speak. The scarcity of literature on the issue and the difficulty of obtaining reliable, valid evidence thus make it impossible to pretend that this report is any more than a beginning, but the effort will have reached its goal if it generates critiques on which to base further empirical work.

# POLITICAL ROLE OF THE INTELLIGENCE AGENCIES IN PAKISTAN

The intelligence agencies in Pakistan affect many aspects of the civilian political system, the political parties, and sectarian violence.

## CIVIL-MILITARY RELATIONS IN PAKISTAN

Because Pakistan's intelligence agencies are instruments of the state, their political role can only be appreciated in relation to the nature of the regime. Understanding civil-military relations is therefore a prerequisite to understanding both their political functions and the mechanisms through which these functions are performed.

Since 1958, Pakistan has endured four military dictatorships, with only brief intervals of civilian regimes between 1971 and 1977, in 1988, in 1999, and, more recently, since the February 2008 elections. Overt military rule is self-evident and needs no particular description. Still, even Pakistan's military regimes have sometimes felt the need to civilianize themselves by co-opting politicians. Such was the case under Ayub Khan and, later, under Zia ul-Haq and Pervez Musharraf. Civil-military relations have therefore always alternated between direct and sometimes brutal domination by the military and power-sharing agreements. Power sharing has, at times, occurred under both civilian and military regimes, the primary difference being the degree of autonomy enjoyed by the civilians.

As observed by the Pakistani political scientist Hasan-Askari Rizvi, Pakistan's power-sharing arrangement means that "the military has important influence over foreign, security and key domestic issues, and mediates confrontations among feuding political leaders, parties or state institutions—if such confrontations are deemed threatening to the political order and stability."[11] The military is obviously the only institution empowered to judge whether such threats exist. Whatever autonomy the civilian government enjoys, for the political and economic management of the state it is always expected to take the military's considerations into account. Thus, every civilian regime is faced with the same dilemma: it has to prove on the one hand that it can act autonomously and is not beholden to the military while, on the other hand, it "cannot afford to alienate the military whose support is crucial for [its] survival."[12] Moreover, the military always ensures, whenever it withdraws from direct rule, that its interests, powers, and privileges are preserved by whatever constitutional safeguards are deemed necessary.

Most of the interests the military considers essential are linked to national security, as defined and controlled by the military. In practice, this means that Pakistan's military has a complete monopoly over nuclear policy, tight control over weapons and equipment procurement, and decisive input on Pakistan's Afghanistan and Kashmir policies. Military officials also expect civilian governments to ensure sociopolitical stability in the country, but they face a constant dilemma. Rizvi notes that "their interests in these matters stem from the assumption that a polity in turmoil cannot sustain a professional military,"[13] but the military can preserve its position and privileges only if the polity is sufficiently weak and divided. This is where the intelligence agencies come into play.

## PAKISTAN'S INTELLIGENCE AGENCIES

There are three main intelligence agencies in Pakistan: Inter-Services Intelligence (ISI), Military Intelligence (MI), and the Intelligence Bureau (IB), although smaller organizations such as the National Accountability Bureau (NAB), abolished in 2008, have also played a role. The MI is a purely military institution, while the ISI is sometimes characterized as "semimilitary."[14] The IB is a civilian agency. For the purposes of this study we will focus mainly, although not exclusively, on the ISI.

*Inter-Services Intelligence.* The Inter-Services Intelligence (ISI) is the best known of the intelligence agencies. Charged with coordinating intelligence among the three military services, the ISI is tasked with collecting foreign and domestic intelligence and conducting covert offensive operations. In this capacity, it is famous for its role in the Afghan conflict through its support of the mujahideen and, later, the Taliban as well as for its involvement in the Kashmir conflict. Its domestic political activities, which range from managing to suppressing political opposition, are, however, less known. Also important is its role in the surveillance of its cadre, foreigners, the media, foreign diplomats accredited to Pakistan, Pakistani diplomats serving outside the country, and the interception and monitoring of communications.[15]

Located in Islamabad, the ISI is reportedly organized into eight divisions:

- Joint Intelligence X (JIX) serves as the secretariat that coordinates and provides administrative support to the other ISI wings and field organizations. It also prepares intelligence estimates and threat assessments.[16]

- The Joint Intelligence Bureau (JIB), also called the "internal wing,"[17] responsible for political intelligence, is the largest division of the organization. Its main responsibility is to gather intelligence on political parties. It also has three subsections that manage operations in India, conduct antiterrorism operations (counterterrorism became an autonomous directorate in the fall of 2007), and provide security to visiting dignitaries. It was supposedly dismantled in November 2008.

- The Joint Counter Intelligence Bureau (JCIB) is responsible for field surveillance of Pakistani diplomats stationed abroad as well as for conducting intelligence operations in the Middle East, South Asia, China, Afghanistan, and the Muslim republics of the former Soviet Union.

- Joint Intelligence/North (JIN) is responsible for Jammu and Kashmir operations, including infiltration, exfiltration, propaganda, and other clandestine operations.

- Joint Intelligence Miscellaneous (JIM) conducts espionage in foreign countries, including offensive intelligence operations.

- The Joint Signal Intelligence Bureau (JSIB), which includes deputy directors for wireless, monitoring, and photos, operates a chain of signal intelligence collection posts along the border with India and provides communications support to militants operating in Kashmir.[18]

- Joint Intelligence Technical (JIT) deals with the collection of all technical intelligence other than communications; with gadgetry; and, possibly, with the subsections involved with explosives, chemical weapons, and monitoring personnel with nuclear weapons roles in Pakistan.

- The Special Wing is responsible for intelligence training for the Pakistan armed forces at the Defence Services Intelligence Academy and possibly for liaison with foreign intelligence and security agencies.

Over the years, the ISI has assumed greater prominence among the Pakistani intelligence agencies. The agency's importance was recognized owing to its role in the Afghan conflict, but it was deeply involved in domestic political affairs long before.

Conflicts between intelligence agencies have, however, occurred during military regimes. They do not necessarily reflect differences on matters of policy—although these may eventually occur—but essentially of personality, turf battles, or both. The reform of the intelligence apparatus carried out by Pervez Musharraf aimed partly at improving the coordination and sharing of burdens among the various agencies.

The ISI was for a long time essentially a federal agency. Because Ayub Khan was reluctant to increase the military budget, neither the ISI nor the MI could post its officers in the districts.[19] The domestic activities of the agencies therefore remained limited. The ISI now has a lieutenant colonel heading a unit in every district of the country and a brigadier, who is in charge of five to six districts, in every major city.[20] A major general heads the ISI's political wing. General Musharraf also created a new body, an intelligence corps, whose officers, after training at the newly created intelligence academy, are meant to serve in the MI, ISI, or both. The idea of the intelligence corps emerged in 1998–1999, and the corps itself became operational in 2000–2001.

*Short history of ISI involvement in politics.* Created in 1948 to focus essentially on India, the ISI comprises the three branches of Pakistan's military: the army, navy, and air force. It originally had no active role in conducting domestic intelligence activities except in Pakistan-controlled Kashmir and the Northern Areas.[21]

The ISI's political role was a direct result of the coup d'état led by the then-COAS, General Ayub Khan, in 1958. The agency at that time became responsible for monitoring Pakistani politicians. Monitoring the media and politically active segments of society also became part of the ISI mission. As a result, "social organizations with potential political influence, such as student groups, trade organizations, and unions [were warned] not to become involved in the political arena"[22] and were kept under tight surveillance. Compared with the situation that developed under and after Zia ul- Haq, who launched an Islamization policy aimed at uniting Pakistan and pressuring the opposition, clerics during Ayub's time were instructed "to leave political rhetoric out of their exhortations."[23]

Relations among the various Pakistani intelligence agencies also changed after Ayub's coup. Although the ISI, MI, and IB each has its own sphere of duty, all have a common goal—preserving national security—a situation that inevitably generates some overlap in their work. In the early years of Pakistan's existence, however, the IB concentrated on domestic political activities while the ISI and MI concerned themselves essentially with military matters. The director of the IB "reported directly to the Prime Minister and the two military agencies to the Commander-in-Chief of the Army. It was left to the Commander-in-Chief to bring all matters of interest to the notice of the Prime Minister through the Ministry of Defense."[24]

When martial law was promulgated in 1958, all the intelligence agencies were placed under the direct control of Ayub Khan, who had become president and chief administrator of martial law. In practice, the intelligence agencies became instruments of consolidation for Ayub's regime, which saw any criticism as a threat to national security. Keen to demonstrate their loyalty to the president, the three agencies began to compete with each other.[25]

This competition did not necessarily improve their effectiveness. The MI and ISI became particularly active on the domestic scene during the 1964 presidential election. They started providing the president with assessments of trends in public opinion. Too eager to please and lacking professionalism, they systematically underestimated the popularity of Fatima Jinnah, sister of Muhammad Ali Jinnah.

The intelligence agencies became even more deeply involved in domestic politics under General Yahya Khan. ISI activities at that time were directed more specifically at ethnic separatists, who were to become a nightmare for successive Pakistani regimes. East Pakistan politicians were among the ISI's first victims, and several were assassinated. A National Security Council was created under the chairmanship of General Yahya Khan himself to control an intelligence operation to ensure that no political party won an overall majority in the 1970 general election.[26] The ISI tried unsuccessfully to infiltrate the inner circles of Sheikh Mujibur Rahman's Awami League, the leading nationalist party in East Pakistan, but the overall operation proved disastrous and the agencies failed to eliminate the Bengali resistance movement.

ISI was also employed by civilian Prime Minister Zulfikar Ali Bhutto against Balochi nationalists and was on occasion no less ruthless than it had been under Bhutto's military predecessors. But in order to counterbalance the ISI, Bhutto also created the Federal Security Force (FSF), a group parallel with the regular police, which operated as a private army "to force his opponents and former allies into submission."[27] More important, however, through an executive order in 1975, Bhutto created the Political Cell of the ISI, which he used unnecessarily to rig the 1977 elections. Bhutto also tried to increase control over the ISI by appointing Lieutenant General Ghulam Jilani Khan, a general he thought loyal to him but who later paved the way for Zia ul-Haq's military coup. These two decisions ultimately brought about Bhutto's downfall.

The FSF was disbanded under Zia ul-Haq, who further expanded the ISI's powers to collect domestic intelligence on political and religious organizations that opposed his regime. The ISI was responsible for collecting intelligence about Sindhi nationalist activities and monitoring the leadership of the Pakistan People's Party (PPP) of Benazir Bhutto, which had launched the Movement for the Restoration of Democracy in the early 1980s. Dissident political leaders were constantly monitored and harassed by the intelligence agencies, in particular the IB and the ISI,[28] but also the Criminal Investigation Agency and the Criminal Investigation Department.[29]

After the success of the Islamic revolution in Iran, the ISI also took on responsibility for controlling the activities of Pakistan's Shi'i organizations.[30] It was also during Zia's reign that the MI, although focused on military and security-related affairs, became involved in domestic political activities. The MI later played an important role in implementing orders to dismiss the two Bhutto-led governments in August 1990 and November 1996.[31]

*Intelligence agencies in Pakistani politics under Pervez Musharraf.* One of the most important and most difficult tasks General Musharraf faced after his coup was to tame the ISI. After September 11, 2001, Musharraf's replacement of General Mahmood Ahmed with Lieutenant General Ehsan ul-Haq as head of the ISI was generally interpreted as a strong signal that he intended to regain control of an agency he thought was too close to the radicals he now intended to fight alongside the Americans.[32] But the timing of General Mahmood's retirement, on October 7, 2001, was coincidental, corresponding with the natural end of his tenure as head of the ISI. Moreover, according to some in Pakistan, Musharraf himself had in the past sent General Mahmood to tell Taliban leader Mullah Omar not to accede to Nawaz Sharif's demand that the Taliban hand over Osama bin Laden, a request expressed through the then–ISI chief, Ziauddin. Several authors, however, argue that General Mahmood made a major mistake when, during a visit to Washington on September 12, 2001, he accepted the "non-negotiable" demands of the U.S. Department of State, demands that would ordinarily have been accepted by Musharraf himself. When Musharraf learned that Mahmood had accepted the demands before he had even been informed of them, Musharraf probably became more suspicious of the ambitions of his subordinate.[33]

Reforms did come to the intelligence agencies. These reforms, however, had much less to do with the ideological convictions of agency leaders than with their willingness to make the entire intelligence apparatus more effective by clarifying the role of each agency, improving their coordination, and optimizing their capabilities. In no way did the reforms reduce the agencies' involvement in domestic politics. All through the campaign leading up to the October 2002 national elections, Benazir Bhutto complained about pre-election rigging by the ISI and coercion against PPP workers.[34] On the other side of the political spectrum, Tehmina Daultana, vice president of the Pakistan Muslim League (Nawaz Group) once described as "a routine practice that the intelligence agencies, which should strengthen national solidarity, are now getting more powers and playing a major role in national politics."[35]

All political parties, not just the opposition, blame the ISI for its interference in Pakistani politics, before and during the time of Pervez Musharraf. Senator Mushahid Hussain, who held the post of minister of information under Nawaz Sharif but by 2002 was very close to Musharraf, felt the need to reform intelligence, asking in particular for a clearer demarcation of each agency's responsibilities and stating that "ISI and MI should be freed from domestic politics, since this is not their job or their mandate."[36] The situation was ironic because Hussain's own party, the Pakistan Muslim League–Quaid-i-Azam Group (PML-Q), had been literally midwifed by the agencies, with the aid of the NAB.[37] Musharraf's subsequent reform of the intelligence agencies partially answered Hussain's first demand, but answering the second remains as unlikely as ever.

The ISI was no stranger during the constitution of the PML-Q, and it openly twisted politicians' arms to join the newly formed "King's party."[38] The agency again played an open role in cobbling together the government of Mir Zafarullah Khan Jamali in 2002, and it rapidly became clear that it would be central to the implementation of the general's political agenda. So even more than it had been under Jamali's predecessors, the agency was given the task, the funds, and the freedom to operate however it wanted.[39] The agency undertook political engineering to weaken the major parties on the one hand and to ensure the complete loyalty of the ruling coalition on the other.[40] Bribes and blackmail were used extensively in both cases. The role of the ISI was particularly obvious in convincing the Muttahida Majlis-e-Amal (MMA) leaders to accept General Musharraf as president in uniform.[41]

Under Musharraf, the ISI also lost a great deal of its secrecy, and its political role became more visible. In March 2003, for example, the *Nation* reported that a dinner had been organized by the ISI at its headquarters for senators of the PML-Q (many of whom it had selected and helped get elected), reportedly "to provide them orientation and get introduced to each other."[42] If the practice was not necessarily new, publicizing it certainly was.[43] In a more formal manner, ISI officials appeared for the first time before the Senate Standing Committee on Defence to brief the committee members about the agency's functions and covert operations. But this did not make the ISI accountable to the Senate.

Although the relationship between the intelligence agencies and Musharraf was sometimes close, it was not without periods of unease. The main intelligence agency especially disliked the free hand Musharraf gave the U.S. Federal Bureau of Investigation to operate within Pakistan. The South Asia Tribune, an online news site, reported at the end of 2002 that the ISI had launched a "whispering campaign"[44] against General Musharraf in the army barracks.

At the end of 2007, despite a deteriorating security situation in parts of the country, monitoring the political opposition seemed to be the main task of the intelligence agencies. Quoting Pakistani security sources, the French newspaper *Le Monde* opined on November 10, 2007, that the military intelligence chief, Nadeem Ejaz (a nephew of Pervez Musharraf's wife), spent more time harassing Musharraf's political opponents than taking care of the security situation in the western provinces of Pakistan.[45]

## HOW ISI SUBVERTS THE POLITICAL SYSTEM

The Soviet withdrawal from Afghanistan in 1989 marked the beginning of a new period of intense political activity for the Pakistani intelligence agencies. Both the MI and the ISI worked hard to implement the military's political agenda, and they have played an active role in every general election since. They have been used to support, oppose, or eventually suppress particular political groups and to aid domestic adversaries of civilian governments with which the military had grown dissatisfied. Intelligence quickly became and remains central for senior commanders pursuing behind-the-scenes political interventions.[46]

The army chief brings information collected by the agencies to the president and the prime minister in a discretionary manner. The president has in the past relied on political intelligence gathered by the agencies to formulate the charges against governments he wanted to dismiss. The army chief therefore controls a very powerful instrument—an instrument that can be used indirectly through the president when civilians are in power, or directly when the military is in power. The latter was the case under Musharraf, to whom the army chief reported.

*Funding political parties.* The military ultimately managed to have Prime Minister Benazir Bhutto dismissed in 1990, and the ISI again became active in the general elections, during which it supported a number of her political opponents.

Allegations of the ISI's interference in domestic politics went public on March 24, 1994, when Mehran Bank president Yunus Habib was arrested for siphoning money from the bank. On April 20, the issue was brought to the floor of the National Assembly by Interior Minister Nasrullah Babar. In 1997, retired air marshal Asghar Khan, former chief of the Pakistan Air Force, filed a Supreme Court petition challenging the legality of a "donation" by the Mehran Bank, a nationalized institution, of some approximately $6.5 million to the then-COAS, General Mirza Aslam Beg, in 1990. The chief justice, Sajjad Ali Shah, called a hearing on ISI's role in domestic politics.

General Aslam Beg, who admitted he had put the money at the disposal of the ISI and MI through a secret service account, had earlier declared that "it was a practice with the ISI to support candidates during the elections under the direction of the chief executive."[47] The money was then used by the MI and ISI for "duly authorized purposes."[48] It was used in particular to fund the Islami Jamhoori Ittehad (IJI), which received a little less than half the total sum. Beneficiaries also included the future prime minister, Nawaz Sharif.[49] A substantial part of the money was also used as "special funds,"[50] destined to finance covert operations.

The 1990 election was not the first instance of ISI involvement in Pakistani politics. Manipulation of elections has been the norm since the creation of the country, particularly under military regimes trying to compensate for their lack of legitimacy. Millions of rupees were embezzled from secret funds for that purpose in 1970 by General Umar, a close associate of Ayub Khan, and N. A. Rizvi, who directed the IB at that time.[51]

Besides the PPP, the only victim of the scandal was the banker, Yunus Habib, who was arrested and jailed. The COAS suffered no judicial consequences and went on the offensive, demanding that legal action be taken against the former chief of the Pakistan Air Force and General Nasrullah Babar for violating the provision of the Official Secrets Act and bringing the armed forces into disrepute.[52]

Although technically still pending before the Supreme Court, the case was de facto suspended by the October 1999 coup d'état of Pervez Musharraf. Almost eight years later, in February 2007, Asghar Khan, one of the main protagonists of the scandal, was still asking the Supreme Court to "determine the role of Inter-Services Intelligence (ISI) in national politics."[53]

Support for particular political groups or parties is not primarily the result of ideological sympathies. Like all individuals, intelligence agents have their own ideological inclinations and political preferences, but these pale in comparison with the military's institutional interest in its own domination of the political landscape. Therefore, support or opposition to any given organization varies over time, the latter being eventually as vicious as the former can be generous.

*Setting up alliances.* In 1988, the ISI, led by Lieutenant General Hamid Gul, set up the IJI, an alliance of right-wing and religious political parties, to prevent Benazir Bhutto's PPP from sweeping the polls.[54] The ISI arranged the reunification of Pakistan's two Pakistan Muslim League factions, which were then joined by smaller organizations, and helped them campaign against the PPP.[55] Imtiaz Ahmed, who was then additional director general of national security at the ISI and as such was involved in all ISI political dealings, launched a campaign to discredit Benazir Bhutto for allegedly working against Punjabi interests.[56] The military opposition failed to prevent a PPP victory in the elections, but ISI manipulations led to greater electoral success for the religious parties, which obtained, collectively, 12 percent of the vote in the 1988 national election, a score they never again reached, including in 2002.

The military high command did not even bother denying its own involvement, nor that of the intelligence agencies, in the process, cynically describing it as "helping to restore democracy." When asked what would have happened if Benazir Bhutto had won the 1988 elections with a greater majority, former COAS General Aslam Beg declared:

> [T]he army perhaps would not have allowed the transfer of power to Benazir Bhutto. There is a strong feeling in the army that Zulfikar Ali Bhutto was responsible for the East Pakistan debacle and that he maligned the army.... So, to ensure that power was smoothly transferred to Benazir Bhutto and democracy restored, the IJI was formed by the ISI. This was done with the clear knowledge that that it would not stop the PPP from forming the government.... I set up a fake competition by creating the IJI to ensure that

a democratic government would be formed.... Let me categorically state that the decision to hold on to or relinquish power rests squarely with the army.[57]

Nonetheless, after the PPP's victory, the ISI never ceased trying to unseat Benazir Bhutto. In October 1989, at the instigation of Hamid Gul and in an operation named Midnight Jackals, the ISI tried to sway PPP members of the National Assembly to back a no-confidence vote against Bhutto and managed to convince the Mohajir Qaumi Movement (MQM; its name was changed later to Muttahida Qaumi Movement) to switch its support from the PPP to the opposition.[58]

But Pakistani intelligence agencies can also initiate rifts within organizations they have created if they find them becoming too powerful or not compliant enough. On several occasions the Jamaat-e-Islami (JI) and the Jamiat Ulema-i-Islam (JUI) have complained about the agencies' developing cracks within the MMA.[59] The Sami ul-Haq faction of the JUI threatened on several occasions to withdraw from the organization at a time when the government was having difficulties convincing the MMA to vote the Legal Framework Ordinance into a constitutional amendment.

*Influencing the media.* Intelligence agencies also influence the political game through the media. The IB has long been known for recruiting informants among journalists.[60] Prominent journalists are also used by the ISI for leaking information whenever the need arises. The MI has used the whole range of instruments at its disposal to ensure silence or complacent coverage.

When journalists refuse to toe the line or probe areas considered too sensitive by the intelligence establishment, it is common for the ISI to threaten them. Journalists have been arrested, brutalized, and in some cases even killed under mysterious circumstances. Intimidation by what the Urdu press calls "sensitive institutions" has been a constant fixture of state-press relations over the years.

In December 2007 when *New York Times* reporter Carlotta Gall inquired about topics that made the government uncomfortable, she was assaulted in her hotel. At the time, Gall was in Quetta, the capital of Balochistan, which is suspected to be a sanctuary for the Taliban under the protection of the military. Men broke into her hotel room; confiscated her laptop computer, notes, and satellite phones; and beat her.[61]

Gall was "lucky" to have been a foreign citizen. Pakistani journalists do not enjoy the same restraint on the part of the agencies, and some of them, such as Hayatullah Khan, have been killed. Khan had been missing for several months before his body was found in the North West Frontier Province. The murder remains officially unexplained, but everyone suspects he was killed by one of the leading intelligence agencies. Other journalists have been held illegally for months, with the government denying any knowledge of their whereabouts until they were eventually released.

Nor do intelligence agencies operate exclusively at the behest of military regimes in Pakistan. Well-known editor Najam Sethi was arrested, beaten, and kept in solitary confinement during Nawaz Sharif's last tenure. Yet the agencies do operate in accordance with what the military establishment regards as the national interest, which it alone defines, irrespective of whether a civilian government is officially in power.

Similarly, tight control over journalists does not mean a complete blackout on information but, rather, very selective information. For years, the so-called liberal press could publish stories about extremist movements and their activities. Journalists writing these stories often enjoyed close connections if not excellent relations with the intelligence agencies, which were more than willing to provide information that exonerated them from any responsibility in the extension and manipulation of these groups. The result was effective manipulation of international public opinion.

*Manipulating political violence.* Divide-and-rule tactics are as old as governance itself, and so is the adage that "the enemy of my enemy is my friend." These dictums are in no way specific to Pakistan's intelligence agencies, but over the years the institutions have developed the peculiar habit of creating enemies for their enemies and then dividing them in order to rule them. Be it the jihadi or sectarian groups or the MQM, the agencies have created a series of Frankensteins whose powers they have had to limit at times by pitting them against each other without trying to eliminate them, but simply making sure that they would remain compliant enough for whatever task they were assigned. In the process, the ISI has created a culture of violence that is likely to be a lasting legacy for the country.

## ISI AND SECTARIAN VIOLENCE

In a December 2002 article on intelligence reform, Senator Mushahid Hussain asked: "Why has sectarian terrorism been allowed to fester and grow since the past 15 years, knowing it is Pakistan's number one internal security threat?"[62] Although the author went on to say that "in the absence of accountability these questions will remain unanswered,"[63] he seemed to imply that the intelligence agencies may have been responsible.

The rise of sectarian violence in Pakistan since the time of Zia ul-Haq finds its roots in the Iranian revolution of 1979, which had a profound impact on the balance of power between the Shi'a community and the Pakistani state, as well as on the relationship between Shi'a and Sunna. In 1979, influenced by the JI, Zia ul-Haq tried to impose *zakat*, a compulsory charity tax deducted by the government. The Tehrik-e-Nifaz-e-Fiqah Jafria (TNFJ),[64] a Shi'a organization created two years after Zia's coup, opposed the measure, which was later abandoned, and challenged the regime. A wave of Shi'a activism soon arose, openly supported by the Islamic Republic of Iran. During the same period, Iran provided funds to Pakistani Shi'a, opened cultural centers in every major Pakistani city, and paid for many young clerics, mostly from the areas of Gilgit and Baltistan, to undertake further study in the cities of Qom and Najaf, where they established contacts with their Middle Eastern coreligionists.[65]

This new Shi'a assertiveness was clearly a challenge for the Zia regime and its attempt to impose Hanafi Islam. As a reaction, the Pakistani dictator decided to employ the most radical Sunni religious groups to squeeze the Shi'a. The first to launch an anti-Shi'a movement in Punjab was the Saudi-sponsored Jamaat Ulema-e-Ahl-e-Hadith (Society of the Ulema of the People of the Hadith), which denounced Shi'ism as a heresy and questioned the loyalty of the Shi'a vis-à-vis Pakistan. This was soon surpassed in violence by the activities of the JUI and the Sipah-e-Sahaba/Pakistan (SSP), created in June 1984 by a member of the JUI from the Jhang district, Maulana Haq Nawaz Jhangvi. Jhangvi was selected by the intelligence community,[66] and he demanded that Shi'a be declared a non-Muslim minority. Despite the SSP's violent activism, however, it always maintained an explicit political profile as it contested elections. In 1995, two SSP leaders became ministers in a PPP-led coalition government.[67]

Soon, Iraq and Saudi Arabia began competing with Iran for influence in Pakistan.[68] The Saudis, in particular, were concerned about the expansion of Shi'a activism and used their vast financial resources to counter it. Part of the money Saudi Arabia provided to Afghan fighters also subsidized militant Sunni organizations in Pakistan, often through the intermediary of Pakistan's military and the ISI.[69]

Until the late 1980s, the SSP limited its activities to the production of hostile literature and public abuse of Shi'a.[70] The subsequent radicalization of sectarian groups was the result of both internal dissent over religious and political issues and the escalation of violence between Sunni and Shi'a movements, resulting in part from the recruitment of criminal elements.[71] While the TNFJ operated as a politico-religious organization, in 1994 the Sipah-e- Muhammad Pakistan (SMP) emerged as the militant wing of Shi'i political activism and the mirror image of the SSP. Although SMP's declared objective was to eliminate sectarianism from Pakistan, its members dedicated themselves to the assassination of political opponents.[72] The SMP distanced itself from the TNFJ when the latter decided to oppose the PPP in the 1988 elections. The SMP leaders thought the decision was opposed to Shi'a community interests and felt that the shift from TNFJ to Tehrik-e-Jafria Pakistan indicated a shift from religion to politics. More important, however, they considered the party was doing nothing to combat the SSP violence.[73]

The creation in 1996 of the Lashkar-e-Jhangvi (L-e-J), a Sunni sectarian terrorist group, was the result of a similar process: a walkout by more radical and extremist elements of the SSP who were protesting what they considered a deviation from Jhangvi's ideals.[74] Throughout the late 1990s, L-e-J claimed responsibility for assassinations of religious leaders, diplomats, priests, and worshippers. It also carried out, in 1999, an assassination attempt on the then prime minister, Nawaz Sharif, who was trying actively to combat the group.[75]

Of particular significance is the fact that Sharif, who decided after a long period of hesitation to combat sectarian violence, did so through the civilian law enforcement apparatus, as he did not expect support from the intelligence agencies.[76] According to Hassan Abbas, when the prime minister requested that the ISI get hold of Riaz Basra, the leader of the L-e-J, he was apparently promised that Basra would soon be apprehended. Instead, the L-e-J stepped up its activities and prepared a terrorist attack against Sharif.[77] During this period, the regional conflicts, in particular Afghanistan because it was a sanctuary for sectarian organizations, fed the militancy.

It would be a mistake, however, to believe that the development of sectarianism in Pakistan was either a purely domestic phenomenon or the sole consequence of foreign influences. These two components were always present, but sectarian forces were tied from the beginning to the Pakistan military[78] and played a role in the domestic political game. The military and its intelligence agencies did not create these components, although the ISI encouraged the formation of the anti-Shi'a Sipah-e-Sahaba,[79] nor did they necessarily totally control them. Rather, these forces have, at times, been used for both domestic and foreign policy purposes.

Domestically, the agencies helped pressure groups or individuals whenever they were found not compliant enough to the will of the master of the moment. As a foreign policy tool, the sectarian forces constituted ideal cannon fodder for causes such as Afghanistan and Kashmir, where, for example, they were always more ruthless than their Kashmiri fellow combatants because, unlike the latter, they had no family ties or emotional link of any kind with the local population and could be used for any dirty operations the agencies could not openly conduct themselves.

Sectarian organizations were officially banned on January 12, 2002, as a consequence of the December 13, 2001, attack against the Indian Parliament, but they did not disappear. The agencies took some steps against sectarian organizations, but the objective of the ISI was to maintain violence at an "acceptable" level, not to eliminate the groups. It divided them, generating infighting every time one organization became too important, and sometimes eliminated uncontrollable elements. One example is that of L-e-J leader, Azam Tariq, who had been allowed to contest the elections from his prison cell in October 2002 despite being charged with murder. He was assassinated on October 5, 2003. His followers had no illusion as to who had killed him, and they intended to demonstrate in front of the ISI headquarters in Islamabad when they were stopped by the police.

This cannot be overemphasized: the intention of the intelligence agencies in Pakistan has been to reduce the importance of the sectarian organizations, not to eliminate them. In March 2006, the Sipah-e-Sahaba was reauthorized to hold public rallies under a new name after a series of negotiations with the ISI.

## ISI AND THE MQM: A CASE STUDY

The Mohajir Qaumi Movement (MQM) emerged on the Pakistani political scene in March 1984 from among the cadres of the former graduates of the University of Karachi known as the All Pakistan Mohajir Students' Organization, which had been established in June 1978.[80] Soon the new organization became a force to reckon with in Karachi, thanks to the availability of weapons owing to the Afghan war and the encouragement of the intelligence agencies, which were trying to curtail the influence of the PPP and Sindhi nationalists.[81] Under the leadership of Altaf Hussain, the MQM soon became a monolithic and violent organization whose terror tactics made Karachi ungovernable.

Although it owed its political existence largely to the military and the generous support of the ISI, the MQM has also been the target of the agency at times. When it became troublesome in the urban centers of Sindh in the late 1980s, the ISI armed some of the

Sindhi nationalist groups to fight the mohajirs and later managed to create a split within the MQM itself.[82] In December 1991, three dissidents of the MQM—Afaq Ahmad, Aamir Khan, and Badar Iqbal—received the support of the ISI, then led by Lieutenant General Asad Durrani, the idea being that "the MQM could be brought to heel only by terrorizing the terrorists."[83] Now two MQM groups soon were at loggerheads.

The split was followed soon thereafter by a direct confrontation between the Altaf faction and the army. In 1992, the army extended an operation initially aimed at dacoits (bands of armed robbers) in rural Sindh to cities known to be MQM strongholds. Subsequently the MQM was forced by the military and the ISI to withdraw from contesting the 1993 national elections. This marked the beginning of the degeneration of the organization. By 1994, the MQM was no more than a label for a number of gangs loosely hanging together.[84] Violence constantly increased, claiming a thousand lives in 1994 alone. Peace was progressively brought back to Karachi by Interior Minister Nasrullah Babar in 1996. MQM continued to decline as a consequence.

The coup d'état of Pervez Musharraf in October 1999 gave the organization new life. In search of political legitimacy, Musharraf regenerated the MQM and attempted to make it a national organization. The MQM benefited in particular from the rigging of the 2002 election, which gave it de facto control of most of urban Sindh. This period was also an era of relative normalization of the MQM, whose terror tactics were temporarily kept in check. The organization's potential for violence remained intact, though, and was reactivated in 2007 when, following a demonstration in favor of the deposed chief justice Iftikhar Muhammad Chaudhry, the MQM organized a counterdemonstration in Karachi on May 12, attacking and killing PPP workers.[85]

Beyond the specific actions of the ISI vis-à-vis the sectarian organizations and the MQM, the relationship between them shows a distorted view of Pakistan's national interest, a view that is often promoted against the interests of the Pakistani population. Figures may differ depending on the authors, but both the sectarian groups and the MQM are responsible for the deaths of several thousand Pakistani citizens.

The cynicism demonstrated in this context by the intelligence agencies is in no way unique and is quite characteristic of authoritarian regimes. What is more surprising and debatable, however, is the impact of the intelligence agencies on the stability of the country and the efficient sustainability of the regime. From this perspective, the rationale for using these organizations appears at the very least to be questionable.

The agencies typically encourage one group to pressure another existing organization, each time generating a new problem that will ultimately have to be dealt with in the same fashion, thus creating a vicious circle partly responsible—one cannot underestimate the impact of the regional conflicts without ignoring the fact that Pakistan is an actor in some of them—for the current disastrous security situation in Pakistan. This situation benefits the regime, however, only as long as it is able to control its various proxies. It becomes vulnerable as soon as the balance created among the diverse organizations supported by the agencies is upset by internal or external factors.

The long-term impact on the state of the intelligence agencies' operations is even more devastating. In most totalitarian or authoritarian regimes, the confrontation between the state and the opposition is direct, not mediated through proxies. In Indonesia and Chile, for example, no matter how ruthless or vicious the repression, the regimes' primary intent was the brutal reaffirmation of the monopoly of the state on legitimate violence. Any state can be occasionally required to use force in the face of specific situations, but when the state itself, as in the case of Pakistan, engages in a proxy war against its own citizens, pitting communities against one another, it turns violence into an acceptable means of managing social and political relations, resulting in a weakened state. In a country where, following decades of indoctrination, jihad (used here in its most common definition of "holy war") is still a romantic notion, this de facto legitimation of violence is destructive to the social and political fabric of an already fragile state and could prove to be political suicide.

## PAKISTAN'S INTELLIGENCE AGENCIES AND THE QUESTION OF DEMOCRATIC CONTROL

The preceding analysis raises a series of questions regarding the definition of the national interest and the authority over security policy in Pakistan. Evidently, it would be naïve to expect a radical change in the intelligence agencies' behavior with regard to politics if dismemberment of their political units were the only reform initiative. The functions that would no longer be accomplished by the internal wing of the

ISI or its equivalent in MI or the IB could easily be performed by another structure or even, in an ad hoc manner, by agents named for a specific task. What must be addressed is the political, constitutional, legal, and, ultimately, democratic control of the agencies.

*Legal and constitutional control of the intelligence agencies in Pakistan.* Two legal channels are supposed to control intelligence agencies in Pakistan:

- The first is the constitution. The superior court hearing a matter must determine whether the power exercised by the agencies is within or beyond their sphere of authorization. A constitutional intervention by the superior court for redress against an intelligence agency would generally occur if the grievance is based on the grounds of excess or abuse of authority.[86]

- The second channel is provided by statutory remedies. The statutory remedies can be ordinary judicial review by processes in existing code (related, for example, to law enforcement) or legislation that creates a special law enforcement force along with investigation-gathering machinery, which automatically includes an appellate process to the superior courts.[87]

Note that intelligence agencies in Pakistan do not have any specific authority granting them extraordinary powers. They operate under the executive powers of the federal government. Intelligence agencies are supposed to work within the general ambit of the federal government's executive powers, contained in Article 90 of the constitution.

Moreover, neither the constitution of Pakistan nor any specific laws provide exemptions or exceptional jurisdiction to the intelligence agencies to undertake any unlawful action against the people present on

Pakistan's territory. All agencies remain under the jurisdiction of regular courts and the general law of the land.[88]

In theory at least, the state cannot, even during an emergency, make laws contrary to the fundamental rights of the people as defined by Article 4 of the constitution, which states that enjoying the protection of the law is the inalienable right of every citizen of Pakistan. It is reinforced by Article 8, which states that laws inconsistent with, or in derogation of fundamental rights, are null and void. No law that benefits intelligence work can infringe on the constitutional rights of citizens of Pakistan. The armed forces and law enforcement personnel more generally cannot be prosecuted for something that is in their domain of service.

The constitution, however, states that the passage of federal laws can be a concern of the IB. In contrast, legislation regarding the MI and ISI, which are entirely controlled by the military, is indirect. Both institutions can be affected only by laws related to defense or security and only through the decisions of the General Headquarters or the federal Interior Ministry.

Similarly, the IB, being a civilian institution, is fully and directly accountable to the constitutional controls by the court. The MI and ISI are not directly accountable. Their respective apex ministries are.[89]

Nevertheless, as government activities, intelligence agency activities must respect the law of the land. In practice, the Supreme Court has the power to make an order if it is convinced that a question of public importance with reference to the enforcement of fundamental constitutional rights is involved. Such cases can be initiated by nongovernmental organizations concerned with human rights, as occurred in the missing-persons case contested by the Human Rights Commission of Pakistan.

*The missing-persons case and limits of judicial control over the intelligence agencies.* In practice, the capacity of the Supreme Court to exercise the full extent of its powers is extremely limited when it comes to Pakistan's intelligence agencies. According to the Pakistani press, the kidnapping and detention of individual citizens without charges is not a new phenomenon in Pakistan; it has been practiced on an unprecedented scale in recent years. During 2006 there were hundreds of newspaper reports of "disappearances" and dozens of accounts of nationalist leaders and activists going missing, particularly in Sindh and Balochistan. The trend continued in 2007. Many of these cases have been registered by the Human Rights Commission of Pakistan, but others are not reported. People released after illegal detention are threatened by the intelligence agencies if they discuss their abduction.[90]

It is, moreover, important to note that the cases under consideration here all have taken place outside of any Pakistani legal framework. The term "enforced disappearance" is used to describe a practice "which implies any form of deprivation of liberty committed by agents of the State, or by anyone acting with the State's authorization, support or acquiescence, followed by a refusal to acknowledge the deprivation of liberty or the concealment of the fate or whereabouts of the person deprived of liberty, which places such a person outside the protection of the law."[91] Since 1974, Pakistan has enacted a number of antiterrorist laws, the last one being the 1997 Anti-Terrorism Act. Their provisions have often been debated on the basis of their impact on human rights. According to the constitution, however, "No person who is arrested shall be detained in custody without being informed, as soon as may be, of the grounds for such arrest, nor shall he be denied the right to consult and be defended by a legal practitioner of his choice."[92]

Examination of available files shows that five categories of people have been detained by the intelligence agencies: journalists, Balochi nationalists, dissidents from Sindh, suspected terrorists, and people with whom the agencies intended to settle scores.[93]

The illegality of the abductions was raised by the political parties long before the chief justice tried to address the issue. In August 2006, the PPP denounced as a national disgrace the "increasing number of citizens of the state [who] not only vanish without a trace but [whose disappearances] are greeted with deafening silence by the agencies."[94] According to the PPP, some 800 people had disappeared during the previous five years without any legal process being followed. Organizations differed on figures; Balochi nationalist parties claim that the number of disappearances was between 3,000 and 4,000.[95] The exact number has, in fact, never been established with certainty. But the opposition kept reiterating the demands for release in the following months.

Cases were also regularly filed in the provincial high courts but without result. Orders of the courts could be effective only with the cooperation of the agencies. In the missing-persons cases, the agencies would simply deny both the kidnapping and any knowledge of the whereabouts of the disappeared. Having no independent means of inquiry, the judges had to content themselves with the answers of the agencies.

In October 2006, the Supreme Court directed the Ministry of Interior and the attorney general of Pakistan to inform the families of the missing persons about their whereabouts and submit a report to the court in the second week of November.[96] Out of forty-one persons who had gone missing, the government declared it had traced nine of them.[97] Cases continued to pile up in the Supreme Court, which kept ordering that reports be submitted to it on the missing persons. The Pakistani press kept reporting about new cases, and human rights organizations kept protesting. From time to time, the agencies discovered the whereabouts of some missing persons—enough to give credibility to their claims that they had nothing to do with the other disappearances.

The crisis of the judiciary inevitably gave a new dimension to the issue. Tensions increased, as did the activism of the Supreme Court. In April 2007, the Supreme Court announced that it would prepare policy guidelines to monitor the role of the intelligence agencies until Parliament legislated on the issue.[98] In June, the court ordered the government to formulate a policy to regulate the functions of intelligence agencies under the law and constitution.[99] In August, it warned the director general of the Federal Investigation Agency, Tareq Pervez, that the agency had to produce the missing persons or go to jail.[100] In October, Chief Justice Iftikhar Muhammad Chaudhry threatened to summon the heads of all intelligence agencies,[101] but he allowed them to regularize the disappearance of the missing persons a few days later, reiterating, however, that the Supreme Court had substantial evidence that those missing were in the custody of the intelligence agencies.[102] The hope of recovering the missing persons disappeared with the imposition of the state of emergency. After the chief justice was dismissed and placed under house arrest, all action stopped. After the February 18, 2008 elections, some of the searches resumed, but no significant results had emerged by the end of 2008.

The illegality of the cases was paradoxically proven a posteriori. In November 2007, against the backdrop of the activism shown by the Supreme Court and following the imposition of the state of emergency, the government passed the Pakistan Army (Amendment) Ordinance 2007.[103] The ordinance, among other provisions, empowered the agencies to detain civilians without pressing any charges and to keep the detainees in custody for an indefinite period.[104] The text was made retroactive to 2003 to cover the cases of the previous years.

In late December 2007, in an apparent attempt to avoid acknowledging the existence of an elaborate secret detention system, the government freed nearly a hundred men suspected of links to terrorism. The "disappeared" had in fact been held in military or intelligence agency cells around the country without being charged, an accusation the government denied.[105]

Only a few from the list of missing persons reappeared. The intelligence agencies knew from the very beginning that without their cooperation with the legal system no traces of the missing would be found and no order of the court could be implemented.

The chief justice could ultimately do no more than raise his voice and make a public noise about the missing persons.

*Past attempts at controlling the intelligence agencies in Pakistan.* Civilian attempts and failures to control the ISI invite the conclusion that no one controls the agencies—they are rogues. This is incorrect. Someone gives orders. Always a practical issue, the problem became public in Pakistan on the occasion of the "Mehran scandal." Having declared that the ISI had always supported political parties, General Aslam Beg went on to say that the so-called political wing of the ISI had been created by Zulfikar Ali Bhutto and that the ISI had become completely free from the army in 1988, being solely under the control of the chief executive.[106] Beg was trying to hold the civilians responsible for the scandal by declaring that as COAS he had merely seen that the money from the Mehran Bank received by the ISI had been used properly.[107] With this declaration, however, he contradicted his claim of civilian control.

General Beg's statement raises a series of questions, all directly or indirectly related to the control of the agency, and all were being asked in the Pakistani press during the Supreme Court hearings. Secret service funds are part of the public exchequer and are provided for a specific purpose. They are theoretically subject to close scrutiny and audits. The director general of the ISI enjoys great discretion in the use of these funds but remains liable to account for every transaction. There are no regulations under which an official can accept a private "donation" for deposit in a secret service account.[108] Who then had authorized a public banker to "donate" public money to a state agency? General Beg's response implied that the civilian chief executive had done so, but then the question was put to General Beg of why the director general of the ISI had to inform the army chief of the transaction as well as of the subsequent use of the money.

The question of the control of the intelligence agencies was also raised in 2006 when six petitions were filed in the Sindh High Court against the illegal detention of political activists by the MI and ISI. The representative of the Ministry of Defence informed the court that the Ministry of Defence had only operational, not administrative control, over the MI and ISI.[109]

This does not mean that the intelligence agencies are under no control. As observed by a former brigadier:

> [T]he Director-General ISI, being a serving General officer, depends on the Military Secretary Branch at the GHQ for his posting, transfer and promotion— everything that has anything to do with his service career. To that extent—and what would be more important than this single factor for the individual concerned—the DG ISI must stay in the shadow of the army chief even if not under his direct command.[110]

The ISI's occasional noncompliance with the civilian leadership's instructions reflects the possibility of conflicting loyalties, but most of the time the service is dedicated to the military. This argument does not exclude the presence of rogue individuals in the system, responsible for occasional mischief outside state control, but it does not make the organization itself a "loose cannon." As a matter of fact, the conflict of loyalty always disappears as soon as the military takes over. The ISI therefore cannot be considered an organization distinct from the military, with a political project of its own. Musharraf himself has dismissed speculation that the ISI might be a "government within the government."[111] ISI operations are part of a larger design, of which the ISI is only an executor. This statement also partly refutes the too-common perception that the ISI is an autonomous rogue institution, as it is sometimes described by the press.[112]

Historically, efforts have been made to limit the powers of the intelligence agencies and bring the ISI in particular under control. Fragile democratic institutions and weak political traditions have been unable to prevent the intelligence agencies from playing an extraconstitutional role. All attempts to monitor the intelligence agencies have failed, leading to the reinforcement of military control over the intelligence apparatus. Civilian leaders have nevertheless tried; they have used essentially two options: naming loyal individuals at the head of the ISI and civilian intelligence agencies and playing on the rivalry among the agencies.

M. K. Junejo, the prime minister chosen by Zia ul-Haq, intended to contain the ISI's influence in order to negotiate a political settlement of the Afghan conflict through the then-ongoing UN-led indirect talks in Geneva. During their "co-habitation" at the head of state, Zia had the ISI spy on Junejo while Junejo had the IB reporting on Zia. Junejo tried to cleanse the IB of army officers.[113] He also tried to replace General Akhtar Abdul Rahman with a more loyal general at the head of the ISI, but he was outmaneuvered by Zia, who imposed Hamid Gul.[114]

The first instance took place during Benazir Bhutto's first tenure as prime minister. It has been written that Shahnawaz Bhutto, son of Zulfikar and brother of Benazir, was poisoned by the ISI in 1985 to intimidate his sister and prevent her from returning to Pakistan, which she did in 1986.[115] She returned, however, willing to rein in the activities of an organization that, according to a commission she appointed to look into its activities, "had all the makings of a de facto government."[116]

Benazir Bhutto's ambition was to reduce the power of the ISI and reorganize the intelligence community and enhance the power of the IB. To do so, she decided to no longer appoint a lieutenant general recommended by the COAS as director general, and she chose Major General Shamsur Rahman Kallue, a retired officer who had been close to her father, to replace Lieutenant General Hamid Gul. She entrusted him with the task of winding up the internal collection role of the ISI and civilizing both the ISI and the IB.[117] Moreover, she tried to introduce an element of competition between the various intelligence agencies by appointing her own loyalists to the Federal Investigation Agency and the IB.

Not only did ISI officials refuse to deal with the newly appointed director general,[118] but Benazir's move also resulted in a reduction of ISI power in contradiction to the intended outcome. General Aslam Beg, then COAS, responded by isolating the ISI, whose director general was no longer invited to the corps commanders' conferences. Covert operations in Jammu and Kashmir as well as in Punjab were transferred to the MI Directorate and placed under the responsibility of the chief of general staff.[119] A number of political assignments, including political surveillance, contacts with politicians, and "developing a strategy to deal with a government with which the Army became increasingly estranged,"[120] were also transferred to the MI.

During her second term (1993–1996), Benazir Bhutto also tried to diminish the powers of the ISI by transferring the responsibility for clandestine operations to the Ministry of Interior, then controlled by a Bhutto loyalist, General Nasrullah Babar, himself an ISI officer during her father's tenure. Benazir was careful, however, not to antagonize the army by pairing Lieutenant General Pervez Musharraf, then the director general of military operations, with Major General Babar in the handling of Afghan operations.[121]

Benazir Bhutto's main political rival, Nawaz Sharif, was not more successful in dealing with the ISI. During his first tenure (1990–1993), he too tried to oppose the COAS, Lieutenant General Asif Nawaz Janjua, by appointing Lieutenant General Javed Nasir as director general of the ISI against the recommendation of Janjua. Nasir in turn was ostracized by the COAS and not invited to the corps commanders' conferences.

During his second tenure (1997–1999), Nawaz Sharif appointed Lieutenant General Ziauddin to be director general of the ISI, against the recommendations of COAS Pervez Musharraf.[122] Like Aslam Beg in the past, Musharraf stopped inviting the director general of the ISI to the corps commanders' conferences. More important, however, he transferred the responsibility for covert operations to the Directorate General of Military Intelligence, then led by Lieutenant General Aziz. The director general of the ISI thus was not part of the planning and implementation of the Kargil operations. The conflict over the control of the intelligence agencies soon led to contradictions in the conduct of the Afghan operations.[123]

All civilian efforts to control the ISI have failed. Except in one instance, however, the resistance seems to have come much less from the organization itself than from the army leadership. Although the director general of the ISI is constitutionally bound to report to the prime minister, the link to the COAS always prevails. When tempted to distance himself from the military institution, the ISI director general is immediately ostracized by the military and his power reduced in favor of the more compliant Directorate of Military Intelligence. The ISI is also immediately marginalized if it shows any loyalty to the elected prime minister. It is interesting that the competition between the various intelligence agencies, in particular the MI and ISI, has never played in favor of the civilians. It has always been the instrument through which the military itself has reasserted its control over the intelligence establishment.

The military has not been purely reactive in this process. According to Hasan-Askari Rizvi, in 1996–1997 the army authorities managed to persuade the caretaker government to induct more army personnel into the IB, giving the MI a greater role in it.[124] The military intelligence establishment has also managed over time to inject many of its officers into civilian intelligence and police institutions. For example, Pervez Musharraf appointed a general, Ejaz Shah, as head of the IB. In addition, under Musharraf, the NAB became a favorite political instrument and was used extensively to charge civilian politicians with corruption. The NAB was, however, underfunded. General Mahmood, then director general of the ISI, proposed to give it funds in exchange for the recruitment of dozens of retired ISI officers, who were thus brought into NAB.[125]

Temptations to counterbalance ISI power were forgotten by successive prime ministers. Even Zafarullah Jamali, who, despite his own political weakness, showed some semblance of independence, took great care to name a former ISI officer acceptable to Musharraf as head of the main civilian intelligence agency, the IB.[126]

CHAPTER

4

# TOWARD REFORM OF PAKISTAN'S INTELLIGENCE AGENCIES?

Although the topic never totally disappeared from the public debate, the issue of reforming the intelligence agencies—or more precisely, the idea that something should be done to rein in the agencies— gained new life after the judiciary crisis, which started on March 9, 2007.

## SUPREME COURT VERSUS INTELLIGENCE AGENCIES

A first attempt by a civilian jurisdiction to rein in the intelligence agencies' political activities came in 2007 from the Supreme Court of Pakistan as it heard petitions filed by the Pakistan Human Rights Commission about the "disappeared," most of whom, despite allegations to the contrary by Pervez Musharraf, were thought to be Balochi nationalists and not jihadis. Like the Sindh High Court, the Supreme Court had been informed in July 2006 by the assistant judge advocate general of the Pakistan Army that the Ministry of Defence had no operational control over the MI and ISI. The government maintained that it had no knowledge regarding the whereabouts of the missing, but it admitted later that it had located some, in effect confirming the absence of parliamentary control over the agencies.[127]

As reported by the *Nation*, "Justice Javed Iqbal [had] hinted at a ruling that [would] provide parliament with guidelines for framing a law to restrain the intelligence agencies."[128] In the wake of the crisis generated by the suspension and later restoration of Chief Justice Iftikhar Muhammad Chaudhry, the Supreme Court felt confident enough to order the release of the missing people. This was one of the reasons invoked by Musharraf to justify the proclamation of emergency and the removal of the chief justice and some of his colleagues.[129] In the absence of any legislative or judicial control, the intelligence agencies remained not out of control but directly answerable to Pervez Musharraf by the sole virtue of his position as COAS.[130]

Newspaper articles describing the intelligence agencies as, for example, being "above the law and accountable to neither the executive nor the judiciary" started to multiply[131] and held the agencies responsible for many of the country's "errors." The agencies, according to *Dawn*, have been "at the forefront of many a strategic depth misadventure, while, on the home front they have been used to subvert the political process, manipulate elections and silence those who disagree with state policy."[132]

## INTELLIGENCE AGENCIES IN THE 2008 ELECTORAL DEBATE

If the documents made public by the political parties when they were in opposition are a reliable indication of their actual agendas, reforming the intelligence agencies should indeed be a priority of the new government. The "Charter of Democracy," signed by former prime ministers Nawaz Sharif and Benazir Bhutto in May 2006 in London, states in Article 32 that:

> [T]he ISI, MI and other security agencies shall be accountable to the elected government through the Prime Minister Secretariat, Ministry of Defence, and Cabinet Division respectively. Their budgets will be approved by DCC after recommendations are prepared by the respective ministry. The political wings of all intelligence agencies will be disbanded. A committee will be formed to cut waste and bloat in the armed forces and security agencies in the interest of the defense and security of the country. All senior posting in these agencies shall be made with the approval of the government through respective ministry.[133]

Similarly, the 2008 Pakistan Peoples Party election manifesto included a provision indicating that "all security agencies, including ISI and MI, will be answerable to the elected Prime Minister."[134]

As the date of the elections approached,[135] criticism regarding the actual and potential involvement of the ISI increased and became an issue in the campaign.

Asad Rehman, from Aurat Foundation Legislative Watch, declared, for example, that "the ISI role in facilitating negotiations with the Pakistan Peoples Party amounts to pre-poll rigging and the ISI is trying to protect the army's role in politics."[136]

The real debate about reform started in October 2007, when Benazir Bhutto demanded the restructuring of the ISI, arguing that the reconciliation process was being destroyed by the ruling Pakistan Muslim League and the intelligence agencies.[137] The then-PPP chairperson remained very cautious, though. She implicitly accused the agency of promoting vested interests and religious extremism but insisted that she was not blaming the ISI as an institution "because there [are] a lot of good people in it" but maintained that the ISI was getting a bad name because "a handful of people had been conspiring against civilian rulers and strengthening the hands of religious fundamentalists."[138] Observing that the agencies have "failed to confine themselves to their legitimate role,"[139] she also insisted that the head of the IB should be a serving police official and not a retired bureaucrat or army officer.

In a context of growing domestic terrorism, Bhutto's argument was real but politically convenient. She was arguing that an intelligence agency that would not spend its time and resources keeping an eye on the political opposition, hounding government critics and dissenters, and keeping the media in check would do a better job of carrying out its actual responsibilities. But introducing the reform of the intelligence agencies to the political debate was not simply politically expedient. Controlling the agencies was a real concern for the former prime minister, not least because she had twice been the victim of their manipulations and she had often discussed the issue in private. Yet, the debate remained limited to two issues only: the nominations of the agencies' heads and the dismantling of the so-called political wing of the ISI.

This last demand became itself a matter of debate when Chaudhry Shujaat Hussain, former interim prime minister and president of the PML-Q, the main political support of Pervez Musharraf, declared that the "political cell" of the ISI should continue to work because "it keeps a watch on political parties and reports their anti-government and anti-state activities."[140] In the process, Hussain attacked his political opponents, in particular Nawaz Sharif, and exposed at once the depth of his democratic conviction and his own links with the agencies. The PPP retorted by reiterating its "demand for the end of the ISI role in the political process," accusing the MI of intimidation and abduction of PPP activists and candidates.

## POST-ELECTION ADJUSTMENTS

Before the February 18, 2008 elections, during the process of relative depoliticization of the army started by the new COAS, Parvez Kayani, it was briefly expected that the army would withdraw its officers from the ISI. The rumor was denied by the Inter-Services Public Relations director general, Major General Athar Abbas, who maintained that the army's presence in the agency was necessary.[141]

In May 2008, after the formation of the new government, the press reported that the intelligence agencies had been instructed to report to Prime

Minister Yousuf Raza Gilani and no longer to Pervez Musharraf. It was also announced that major structural changes were being made, some of which involved the ISI political wing's being made part of the MI.[142] Neither announcement has been confirmed thus far, nor is it clear what democratic benefit the shift of the ISI political wing to the MI would bring. Later in May 2008, the PPP announced that it would soon take legislative action to disband political wings of all intelligence agencies.[143]

Until the end of July 2008, reform seemed to be limited to changes at the head of the main agencies, reflecting the new power structure in Pakistan. As president and COAS, Pervez Musharraf had concentrated the control of the IB, ISI, and MI in his own hands, the latter by virtue of his position as COAS. He had further reinforced this control by nominating family members or staunch loyalists to leading positions. Brigadier Ejaz Shah, a close friend, was heading the IB; Musharraf's nephew, Lieutenant General Nadeem Taj, was director general of the ISI; and Lieutenant General Nadeem Ejaz was director general of the MI.

Pervez Musharraf lost control of MI to his successor when he resigned his position as COAS. The new head of the military, Parvez Kayani, soon appointed his own man, Lieutenant General Mohammad Asif. Nadeem Taj remained director general of the ISI for a few more months, even after Musharraf's departure from power. He was later replaced by Lieutenant General Shuja Pasha. The nomination signaled no more than a gradual assertion of power by the COAS. The IB is now headed by Tariq Lodhi, close to Asif Ali Zardari, leader of the PPP. Other controversial intelligence officials, such as Sindh operational head of the ISI, Brigadier Tariq Huda, have also been removed from their positions. Considered the de facto chief minister of Sindh, Huda was said to have been in charge of, among other things, the May 12, 2007, operation to block the entry into Karachi of Chief Justice Iftikhar Muhammad Chaudhry, a decision that resulted in the deaths of dozens of people.[144]

More interesting, however, was Parvez Kayani's decision to dismantle the so-called political wing of the ISI on November 25, 2008. Such a decision had been a recurrent demand—without any success whatsoever— of the PPP both in opposition and in government. The situation changed in the fall of 2008 when Pakistan suddenly found itself under strong international pressure to rein in the ISI following the attack on the Indian embassy in Kabul, for which the entire international community held the intelligence agency responsible. It then became convenient to eliminate a structure whose function could easily be performed outside any formal mechanism. Parvez Kayani thus diminished international pressure by trying to persuade the international community that the ISI had effectively withdrawn from politics and that the civilian government was in charge. Thus, the civilian government was designated as responsible for a security policy over which it still had no control. Fundamentally, however, the system changed only marginally.

## PROSPECTS FOR REFORM

In such a situation, the need for reform appears increasingly urgent, but its prospects are limited. The civilian government seems to be trying to make the

ISI more accountable and has taken several steps to reduce its power. The agency budget is now discussed by Parliament. The government also holds regular security briefings involving not only cabinet members and intelligence officials but also the entire security apparatus. The intention is to assert control over the intelligence agencies by building a national consensus through Parliament. The forthcoming elections to the various parliamentary committee chairmanships will be decisive in this regard.

It would have been naïve, however, not to expect strong resistance from an organization that has never accepted democracy. The series of terrorist attacks that have taken place inside and outside Pakistan (in Kashmir, Afghanistan, and the Federally Administered Tribal Areas of Pakistan) in which responsibility of the ISI is increasingly acknowledged can be interpreted as evidence of its willingness to increase the vulnerability of the democratic government.

The tension between the two institutions is already obvious, as demonstrated by an incident on July 26, 2008. On that date the prime minister's office made a surprise announcement that the ISI and the IB would immediately be placed under the administrative, financial, and operational control of the Interior Ministry, headed by Rehman Malik. The decision was, however, reversed less than 24 hours after it was announced. The government's Press Information Department issued a statement saying the government had meant only to reemphasize "coordination between the Ministry of Interior and the ISI in relation to the war on terror and internal security."[145] Similar terms were used by the entourage of Pervez Musharraf. However, the Pakistani press reported on July 28, 2008, that the prime minister, then in London, was informed by a phone call in the middle of the night "that the Army, and especially the ISI, was trying its best to stay out of politics for the past many months but his decision to place the ISI under the control of Rehman Malik would be seen as an attempt to again politicize the ISI for achieving certain political objectives."[146]

That the government had actually tried to confront the ISI in such a way is surprising. Putting the agency under the Interior Ministry made no sense, although some analysts suggest that "the move would have opened up the ISI's finances and operations to scrutiny," as asserted by Ayesha Siddiqua Agha.[147] The risk of a coup would have been real. The government explanation of a miscommunication seems, therefore, plausible. But it seems also likely that the government was trying to remind the intelligence agency that it had to conform to government direction and coordinate its operations with the Interior Ministry.

The fact that opposition senator Mushahid Hussain of the PML-Q denounced the attempted shift of ISI management as politicization and argued that putting the ISI under the Interior Ministry would "seriously undermine national security"[148] shows that the ISI will also use politics to resist any attempt by the civilian government to control it.

The story immediately became an embarrassment for the prime minister, who was seen as unable to assert his control over the agency. He could not ignore what seems to have been a veiled, nevertheless real, threat from the army. The incident showed publicly that the agencies were running contrary to the government's policies and, despite the Pakistani constitution, the power of the prime minister over the ISI remained nominal. The episode may have further weakened the chances of actual reform of the ISI.

## WESTERN DILEMMAS

The cooperation between Western intelligence agencies and the ISI could also prove a considerable obstacle to reform. Although this cooperation has always proved deeply frustrating, most ISI partners prefer flawed cooperation to no cooperation at all. Partners keep interacting directly with the ISI, depriving the Pakistan government of its leverage but putting pressure on it to deliver high-value targets who are either under ISI control or who would have to be identified and arrested by the ISI. If there are legitimate questions about the ability of the government to assert its control over the ISI in the future, the current policy carries its own contradiction. Western governments may not be willing to gamble on the ability of the current government to increase its authority, but the security of the region, and by extension the security of the West, requires civilian ownership of Pakistan's foreign and security policies. There is no good answer to the dilemma, but policies whose undesired impact is to diminish the authority of the elected government are counterproductive and could become an impediment to the implementation of much needed reforms.

# DEMOCRATIC CONTROL OF INTELLIGENCE AGENCIES IN TRANSITIONAL DEMOCRACIES

Common wisdom about Pakistan states that the polity is so weak and so corrupt, the military so entrenched in the political process and so essential for the country's unity and survival, and the intelligence agencies so strong that any change other than the marginal is simply impossible. Although exaggerated and sometimes debatable, each of these assertions contains an element of truth. The judiciary crisis—the refusal of one man, Chief Justice Iftikhar Muhammad Chaudhry, to legitimate the dictatorship—demonstrates the fragility of the entire edifice, however, and it opens a window of opportunity for structural changes deeper than the current redistribution of power.

Yet there is no magic formula to transform overnight an authoritarian regime into a full-fledged democracy nor to suddenly prevent intelligence agencies from targeting political opponents. Changes in the formal legal structures are only part of the answer if the law is to reduce the powers of the institutions that control the implementation mechanism. Reforms will bring about change only if they reflect the actual balance of power within the country.

Yet countries where the military has been as important an actor in political life as it is in Pakistan have managed to reduce the power of both the military institution and of the intelligence agencies. It may thus be useful to look at the democratic transition experienced by two other states—Indonesia and Chile—where the army enjoyed a similarly dominant position and where the intelligence agencies were an equally ruthless instrument of power. In Indonesia and Chile the establishment of democratic control over the intelligence agencies remains incomplete, imperfect, and in some respects flawed. Yet both countries have come a long way since the days of their dictatorships and, although there have been instances of abuse by the agencies, their behavior has improved significantly.

## INTELLIGENCE REFORM IN INDONESIA

Indonesia has undergone significant reforms in its civil-military relations, especially since the late 1990s. The country's institutions are now reflecting the ascendance of civilian leadership although reforms need to be broadened and improved.

*Civil-military relations and structure of the Indonesian intelligence agencies in Suharto's Indonesia.* In Indonesia, the military enjoyed a dominant role after independence in 1945 but became the country's premier institution in 1966, when it assumed a central position. Even since the fall of Suharto in May 1998, a significant number of cabinet positions have been occupied by serving or retired generals, while active and retired officers have occupied seats in the People's Legislative Assembly (Dewan Perwakilan Rakyat) and the People's Consultative Assembly (Majelis Permusyawaratan Rakyat), the supreme governing body.

Besides its direct political influence at the national level, the military also maintained a regional and local infrastructure through territorial commands spread throughout the archipelago. This allowed the military to exert constant political pressure everywhere in the country. In strategic terms, the territorial commands were justified by an Indonesian defense doctrine based on withdrawal to the hinterland, during which the territorial forces would mobilize the population in a guerrilla resistance against any potential invader, as they had during the war of independence.[149] In practice, however, the defense of the territory was a lesser concern than internal security and stability. But if the expansion of the territorial forces was inspired in the 1950s and 1960s by the strength of the Communist Party of Indonesia (PKI) and a series of separatist movements, this mandate soon expanded to social control of the entire archipelago.

Damien Kingsbury notes, "Since the mid-1960s, Indonesia has been a state with military personnel, not a state with a military government."[150] Even though

Suharto sought to prevent the military from becoming an independent political actor, the military always enjoyed a considerable degree of administrative freedom. This freedom applied to the institution itself, in particular with regard to the appointments of lower- and middleranking officers. But its role extended far beyond a simple presence in the government, as asserted by its doctrine known as "dual function," in which the Indonesian military presented itself as both a defender of the state and "an active component of the social and political life of the state."[151] As a defender of the state, the military's focus on actual or perceived internal threats rather than the stated invasion threat made it a highly political instrument. Its institutionalized social and political role, materialized by the insertion of officers into positions held in other countries by civilians as well as into key positions in the decision-making structures, was reinforced during most of the dictatorship by close ties between President Suharto and the leading generals.[152]

Born out of a coup that led to the massacre of at least half a million people suspected of belonging to the PKI, the New Order regime of President Suharto first worked at consolidating itself. This consolidation provided an immediate argument in favor of a strong military, but it was further rationalized by the "geopolitical concern that communist infiltration during the cold war would escalate communist subversion,"[153] which also convinced officers of the prominent role of the defense forces in maintaining national integrity.

Suharto then intended to turn Indonesia into a center of foreign investment, making economic and social development the nation's first priority and providing the military with a rationale that identified political stability as a precondition for development.[154] The length of the initiative, measured in decades, ensured the prospect of long-term military control of politics. But if the country's development was the core ideological basis of the New Order regime, Suharto's concepts of a unitary state and a "greater Indonesia," which made the country the successor state of the Netherlands on all the area's territories previously occupied by the former colonial power, were also powerful arguments to convince the military to support the new regime.

In practice, this meant controlling labor organizations, political parties, Islamic movements, and separatist movements most active in East Timor, Aceh, and West Papua (Irian Jaya) but also in Maluku. Strong-arm tactics were routine. Suharto's control was asserted through intimidation, intelligence investigation of political opponents, and tight control over politics. Torture, extrajudicial killings, and illegal imprisonment became the norm in order to prevent the reemergence of the PKI in the first phase; and these methods were used against whoever looked like a threat to the regime or whose activity implied a risk of destabilization in part of the country in the second phase. In the second phase, the military regularly insisted that it had not achieved complete stability, thus reasserting the need for its constant intervention in politics. In this context, strong intelligence agencies and the regime itself were consubstantial.

The intelligence organizations that came to dominate Indonesia had been created before the New Order era, but Suharto gave them a new role and importance in the political system. Besides the armed forces and the national police, the intelligence service formed the third pillar of Indonesia's security apparatus, bringing the entire population under de facto surveillance. In the area of political control and repression, the activities of the intelligence organizations were more akin to the actions of a police force in a totalitarian state. They acted partly as a visible deterrent but also as an overt force for social control.[155] Intelligence gathering itself had much more to do with the activities of individuals and groups for political purposes than with the gathering of information on the activities and interests of foreign governments, supposedly the raison d'être of intelligence agencies.

Although intelligence functions were performed by a plethora of organizations, two agencies clearly stood out: The Strategic Intelligence Agency (Badan Intelijen Strategis [BAIS]), responsible for military and foreign intelligence, and the State Intelligence Coordinating Board (Badan Kordinasi Intelijen Negara [Bakin]).

BAIS, which operated domestically and abroad, was the most important military intelligence agency in Suharto's Indonesia and an internal part of the structure of the armed forces of Indonesia (known by the acronym TNI). Sitting atop the army's structure of intelligence, BAIS reported directly to the commander in chief, who decided what information should be forwarded to the president. BAIS was at the peak of the intelligence structures of the four separate services. BAIS was a "centralized operational intelligence gathering body, articulated with the operational resources of the Armed Forces Commander."[156]

Under Suharto, BAIS was highly oriented toward political analysis, in line with the general concern of the armed forces for social engineering and social control. BAIS agents reached into every area of society, and the agency's permission was required for everything from appointment to high government office to admission to the military academy. The armed forces commander in chief was also chief of BAIS. Closely integrated with the army's Social and Political Affairs and Territorial Staff structure, and with the Social and Political and Special Directorates of the Department of the Interior and the office of the Deputy Attorney General (intelligence), BAIS operated on the entire archipelago, monitoring all social conditions considered significant.[157] Its close relationship to the army's territorial presence, down to the village level, gave it an exceptional capacity for surveillance and intervention. The organization was known to "employ torture and abuse of legal rights on an administrative basis."[158]

Bakin was established in 1967. It has been called a type of "military dominated secret police"[159] although it was a nominally civilian organization. Although it employed civilians in its middle and lower ranks, all four senior deputies were active-duty or retired officers. The preeminent intelligence body of the regime, Bakin was known for its "black operations," but it lost some of its domestic operational role and authority to BAIS.[160] It nevertheless played a key part in the maintenance of the system of surveillance and repression. Its primary targets were initially the political parties, the dissidents, and the Chinese community, especially those in the Chinese community thought to be planning a communist revival.

Both organizations staffed a third body, the Agency for the Coordination of Support for National Stability Development (Bakorstanas), led by the armed forces commander, which monitored political activities to prevent any political threats to the regime. Bakorstanas succeeded Kopkamtib, a body created to handle the massive arrests that followed the 1965 abortive coup,[161] and it was used in effect to suppress political opposition through its authority to intervene "in the interest of political and social stability."[162] Under an instrument called Litsus (search, scrutiny), it could inquire about anyone and could, for example, intervene in strikes and other labor actions or screen candidate lists at every level to determine whether candidates had been involved in the 1965 abortive coup or posed real or imagined security risks. After the fall of Suharto, Bakorstanas was disbanded, but its staff remained in their home agencies.

Of particular importance was also the political and social control of the population that was imposed by the territorial command structure. The army was and is organized in centralized and territorial commands. The territorial command, which employed about 140,000 personnel spread across the entire archipelago, complemented the civilian administration at each administrative level. It is subdivided into eleven regional commands, or Kodams, headed by major generals and subdivided into subregional commands, Korem, headed by colonels and based in the major towns of each region.

Army control was doubled by another intelligence network, not only at each administrative level, but also at the street level. Within the village itself, group or street chiefs reported to a higher echelon (kepala/ desa), which reported to a higher echelon (lurah), then to the camat, bupati,[163] and finally to the governor, who reported to the central government. This social control over every single aspect of individual life (including the most intimate) was independent of the intelligence agencies.

The territorial structure soon became the major instrument for keeping the Suharto regime in power. Territorial troops were used to monitor and control the activities of all nongovernmental organizations, political parties, student groups, religious organizations, and trade unions.[164]

The institutionalized basis of the intelligence apparatus was in place as early as 1966, and it made a crucial contribution to the durability of the New Order regime. It included overt intelligence agencies, both civilian and military, as well as the intelligence bodies of the army, navy, air force, and police. Government departments such as the Department of Labour Affairs, the Ministry for the Reform of the State Apparatus, and the Attorney General's Department, also had intelligence divisions. Of particular importance was the Directorate for Social and Political Affairs of the Ministry of Interior. In addition, there were also coordination and command organs such as Kopkamtib and its successor, Bakorstanas, as well as ad hoc intelligence and combat sections of special military forces, "a varying cohort of looser and less bureaucratically standardized and legally authorized groupings of state officials, gangsters and hired goons, suborned or hired intellectuals and other such informers and enforcers."[165]

*Political background of the reforms.* The reforms
of the intelligence apparatus decided after the
resignation of Suharto did not take place in isolation.
They were part of a larger process of democratization
and demilitarization of the state.

Indonesia's democratic transition was precipitated,
however, by the consequences of the Asian financial
crisis of July 1997. The depreciation of the Indonesian
rupiah caused widespread defaults on loan payments
and steep increases in the prices for basic goods. Riots,
including student protests, multiplied throughout the
archipelago. Students were at the forefront of the revolt,
demanding first that the government address the crisis
and later calling for Suharto's resignation, the end of
the military's "dual function," and "full-fledged
democratization."[166]

The democratization process was also the result of
the initiatives of reform-minded military officers who
believed it was no longer tenable to maintain the old
position of the military.[167] Their ideas were formalized
in a reform program called the New Paradigm, which
constituted the framework through which the TNI was
to achieve the separation of the armed forces from
civilian and political functions. It included the
separation of the police from the armed forces, the
end of military involvement in local political affairs,
the transformation of the Office of Social and Political
Affairs into an Office of Territorial Affairs, the end of
the social and political role of the armed forces in
political affairs down to the local level, the end of the
appointment of military officers to civilian positions
in central and regional governments and the
requirement that officers chose between military and
civilian careers, the removal of the influence of the

military from day-to-day politics, the reduction of the number of seats reserved for the armed forces in Parliament, and the neutrality of the military in politics.[168] Despite the fact that the New Paradigm had been discussed long before the fall of Suharto, it was not until the resignation of the dictator that real public debate could begin.

The military itself was divided over the issue. Commander General Wiranto and Major General Yudhoyono, the chief of staff of sociopolitical affairs, convinced the aging dictator to step down, but they were up against hard-line elements of the armed forces such as Suharto's own son-in-law, Prabowo Subianto, and former armed forces commander Feisal Tanjung. They had tried to convince Suharto to declare martial law and were prepared to mobilize militant Islamic networks in Suharto's defense.[169]

Suharto resigned from the presidency on May 21, 1998. His successor and former deputy, Jusuf Habibie, found himself under strong domestic and international pressure and felt he had little choice but to embark on a program of liberalization. Under pressure from Indonesian society, Wiranto and Major General Yudhoyono initiated a series of reforms that considerably reduced the role of the military in government along the lines of the New Paradigm. The reduction of military representation in Parliament, initiated reluctantly by Suharto, continued under Habibie.

The position taken by the military was met with considerable ambivalence. Most Indonesians resented the long history of atrocities perpetrated by the armed forces under Suharto as well as the deeply entrenched position of the military in the state's economy. However, the government's refusal to use force against popular protests granted Suharto some public approval and increased the personal popularity of some military leaders.

The armed forces leadership later acknowledged that its social and political role was too large in comparison with its defense responsibility. Active military officers serving in civilian positions had to choose between service with either the military or the civilian government. Politically, the links with the government party, Golkar, were severed.[170] The military presence in Parliament ended: until the mid-1990s, the military held 100 seats in Parliament, but this number decreased to 75 in the last years of the Suharto regime and was further reduced to 38 after his fall from power. The remaining presence of the military in Parliament was ended in 2004.

The degree to which the reforms succeeded in actually severing the link between the military and politics is often questioned. If the army has effectively given up all positions in Parliament and remained remarkably neutral in the elections (with the exception of East Timor in 1999), it has retained and extended its role in conflict areas, maintained its influence in local affairs, and is still a force to reckon with in day-to-day politics.[171] Nevertheless, the reforms constituted the background against which the redefinition of the intelligence agencies took place. They were perhaps less significant in their actual content than in symbolizing deeper societal and political change. As such, they signaled the beginning of a new era in which past quasi-totalitarian practices no longer had their place.

*Institutional changes.* A first important step in weakening the legal basis of the repressive interventions of the Indonesian intelligence system was the abolition of the 1963 Anti-Subversion Law by the Habibie administration in April 1999. Also during the Habibie administration, army special forces command officers who had committed crimes connected to the abduction and torture of political activists were prosecuted and convicted. The end of impunity constituted a major step in reducing the use of terror by state agents.[172] The removal of the police force from the army command structure was also mandated during Habibie's tenure.

Still, the major institutional changes in the Indonesian intelligence apparatus took place during the presidency of Abdurrahman Wahid. Committed to the principle of civilian supremacy and motivated by the need to secure his own position against military pressure, the new president limited considerably the capacity and freedom of action of the agencies, although it should be recognized that he had not come to power with a plan to reduce military power.[173] In March 2000, in a move supposedly aimed at promoting civil society and human rights principles, President Wahid decided to disband Bakorstanas.[174] Its intelligence functions were transferred to the Badan Intelijen Negara (BIN; the new state intelligence agency and the successor to Bakin), and the organization itself was liquidated. Some of Bakorstanas's personnel were reallocated to other military positions, but some were simply fired. As a consequence, procedures of "special investigation" that allowed extrajudicial action by Bakorstanas were also liquidated.[175] Similarly, the Directorate of Social and Political Affairs of the Ministry of Interior was disbanded.[176]

On April 17, 1990, Abdurrahman Wahid also abolished Presidential Decree No. 22. In practice, this meant that civil servants, politicians, and state officials, who previously had been screened to check whether any were members of the PKI or any other illegal organization or were linked through their relatives or by association, were no longer subject to such a screening procedure before assuming their new posts. Similarly, job seekers were no longer obliged to produce documents attesting to their good conduct.[177] Most of the archives compiled by Bakorstanas were destroyed following its dissolution.

The civilian leadership also reasserted its power through the nominations at the head of the military. The upper echelons were replaced by more compliant officers. In addition, the minister for defense and security agreed to a request from the International Monetary Fund and the World Bank for an audit of the extrabudgetary funds of the military.[178]

Organizational changes have remained limited although not negligible. During the Suharto era, BAIS, the military agency, was the more important of the two intelligence organizations. It exercised extensive vertical authority through the TNI, often bypassing the chain of command, although it lost some of its prerogatives and powers in 1994 when it was renamed, downsized from eight to five directorates, and no longer under the direct command of the armed forces commander in chief. Under the Wahid administration, BAIS regained its pre-1994 status and importance. The new structure has seven directorates and three operational units.[179]

Since Suharto's time, however, the civilian BIN is officially preeminent although this is debatable in practice because BAIS is a much more professional organization. The Wahid administration not only changed its name from Bakin to BIN; it also increased its budget with the intention of emphasizing its operational function and diminishing the coordinating role that it had no longer really been exercising since the last years of the Suharto regime.[180] This reflected the difficulties Abdurrahman Wahid was experiencing in obtaining intelligence material from BAIS and Bakin.[181] The new president frequently complained of being deprived of intelligence from the state agencies. This lack of information was also a response to changing intelligence needs, as the failure to prevent the bombing of the Jakarta stock exchange demonstrated in 2000. Nevertheless, these changes primarily reflected the shift of emphasis from domestic to external threats and a new sense that foreign forces were at work to dismantle Indonesia.

Under Suharto, all intelligence agencies reported to the president, with the head of BIN nominally in charge of coordination among the agencies. This integration was, in fact, never totally realized. After the fall of Suharto, President Habibie created the National Defense Stabilization Council, which consisted of most of the important members of the cabinet in another guise, but he virtually abandoned any attempt at serious coordination. Today, BAIS reports to TNI headquarters while BIN and the police are "nondepartmental institutions," meaning that they do not belong to a ministry and, thus, report directly to the president. BIN's head is, moreover, the president's chief intelligence adviser. Parliament also has an oversight function over the agency.[182]

*Coordination deficiencies.* The fact that two of the main intelligence organizations are under the direct responsibility of the president should have theoretically made the coordination between them easier. In practice, though, there is no executive authority to arbitrate between the agencies. Despite the restructuring of the intelligence apparatus, coordination has hardly improved.

Partly the result of a somewhat traditional interagency rivalry, the two agencies generate an unnecessary duplication of work and contribute to blurring the lines of authority and, consequently, a de facto autonomy of the agencies, which inevitably limits the effectiveness of any democratic oversight. Three agencies, BIN, BAIS, and the national police, are involved in collecting and analyzing information related to domestic security, meaning that in practice all three deal with terrorism in addition to their more specific assignments.

*Parliamentary oversight of the intelligence system.* Parliamentary oversight was also introduced by President Wahid. Three commissions are particularly relevant from the point of view of democratic control of the intelligence agencies: Commission I is in charge of defense, TNI, foreign affairs, and intelligence; Commission II deals with law enforcement; Commission III is in charge of police.

In practice, however, things are not as clearly defined as suggested by the commissions' attributions. Law enforcement comes, as indicated, under Commission II but if law enforcement implies the use of force, it falls under Commission III. In effect, the control exercised by each commission over the institutions each is charged with monitoring is nominal. Control is exercised through the budget and is indirect for BAIS, whose budget comes from the TNI. Control is direct for BIN, which receives its money directly from the state. Parliament can, of course, approve, reject, or curb the budget proposed by each institution, but there is no control on the way the budget is actually spent. More significant perhaps is the fact that, unlike civil society, parliamentarians seem to remain only marginally interested in the intelligence issue or are unwilling to antagonize the agencies.

*Democracy, terrorism, and reform of the intelligence agencies in Indonesia.* In Indonesia, as in most countries, the need to combat terrorism has created tension between the need to strengthen still very fragile democratic controls and the necessity for reinforcing the analytical and operational capacities of the intelligence agencies. Wahid's successor, Megawati Sukarnoputri, had been strongly criticized for the lack of intelligence cooperation before and after the bombing in Bali in 2002. She immediately tried to restore the coordinating function of BIN. Similarly, she tried to reinforce the agency's operational functions, but subtle and cautious shifts in policy had been initiated even before the Bali bombing as the Indonesian authorities were becoming increasingly aware of an Islamic terrorist threat on their own soil.

Radical Islamist groups such as the Lashkar Jihad, whose leaders publicly promoted jihad against Christians, enjoyed the support of some Indonesian power centers. Politicians long refused to acknowledge the reality of the problem. In 2001, when Philippine authorities arrested and tried Indonesians for alleged complicity in international terrorism, the response of part of the political class in Indonesia was to denounce the framing of its citizens. The claim by the head of BIN, Lieutenant General A. M. Hendropriyono, a former special forces officer, that foreigners had trained with Lashkar Jihad was met by similar reactions.[183]

The tension between democratic control and operational capabilities became obvious and took a more serious turn when Hendropriyono tried to use the presidential instruction of October 2002 to have extensive police powers granted to BIN.[184] The attempt was unsuccessful, but a draft intelligence law, in preparation since September 11, 2001, was leaked. The law, still pending in Parliament, was immediately attacked by human rights organizations for denying basic rights to detainees and violating Indonesian criminal law and international human rights law.

Among the major concerns were the vagueness of the legal standards, the lack of a provision defining a role for the judiciary in the oversight of BIN's activities, and the absence of clearly defined lines between criminal investigations and intelligence activities. The possibility for BIN to move into law enforcement and to arrest people for up to seven days and detain persons for up to thirty days without any judicial oversight or control, access to counsel, and the filing of criminal charges was seen as particularly threatening to civil liberties. The vague and broad definition of the notion of "threat to the nation" was also seen as using the law "to target peaceful political activists, opposition parties or groups, and indigenous groups."[185]

Although the intelligence law is still pending, BIN expansion was authorized by Megawati Sukarnoputri in 2004.[186] The transfer of some police intelligence functions to BIN after the September 2004 bombing of the Australian embassy in Jakarta raised concerns similar to those generated by the draft intelligence law.[187]

The restructuring of BAIS, the military intelligence agency, was also subject to strong criticism although for different reasons. Opponents were notably uncomfortable with a greater military intelligence presence at a time of democratic change. Some blamed the agency for the increased conflict in Indonesia, accusing BAIS operatives of provoking unrest to underline (and resuscitate) the role that the military had long played in Indonesia's politics.[188] BAIS reports on political, economic, social, cultural, security, and defense matters, both foreign and domestic, and there is suspicion that it may be pursuing its own agenda.

Richard Tanter, in his work on Suharto's intelligence apparatus, wrote that "the instruments of state surveillance are multiple, confused, and for much of the population, probably low level, passive and somewhat ineffective."[189] The same comment could be made about today's intelligence services. The "totalitarian ambition" described by Tanter about an earlier time has indeed disappeared, and a progressive change in the role of the intelligence agencies has been observed, but the broader political changes within Indonesia are responsible for the changes within the intelligence agencies.

First, as observed by Damien Kingsbury, "since the fall of Suharto, internal intelligence activity has slowed in part because successive governments have been less paranoid and thus less concerned to exercise a tight grip on the political process."[190]

This change, in turn, has had a negative impact. The new situation of the intelligence system is characterized by a lesser, not a greater, degree of government control. The lack of bureaucratic strength—defined as the ability to develop coherent policies and then implement them as well as the near-absence of interdepartmental coordination—favors the compartmentalization of the intelligence function and real autonomy for each agency at the provincial and local levels, allowing agencies to define their roles themselves to a great extent.

Ten years after the change of regime, many important issues have not been tackled or have been addressed only marginally. The legal basis of the entire system is weak and sometimes nonexistent. Relations with Parliament and within the larger intelligence community—the lines of authority and the respective tasks of each agency—still have to be defined.

These issues have been partly corrected by the political dynamic of the democratic transition. The transition to a more traditional role for the intelligence agencies is also the result of the withdrawal of the military from politics and of a more politically pluralistic society. The climate of change in Indonesia has made traditional intelligence functions, as experienced by the population under the New Order regime, far less politically acceptable. As a consequence, the process has not resulted in a real assertion of control by civilian governments over the intelligence agencies.

The situation of the intelligence agencies is affected by the political culture of a country where government officials consider that all institutions are instruments of the development of the nation. The use of the intelligence agencies in such a context is therefore only as "democratic" as the country's leadership; it does not result from actual constitutional balances and checks. The failure of the Yudhoyono administration to investigate and explain the murder of Munir Said Thalib, a human rights activist who was poisoned on a flight from Jakarta to Amsterdam in 2004, demonstrates that ten years after Suharto's downfall, the elected government still does not have full control over the intelligence agencies and that the agencies' involvement in politics is not really over. Munir's criticism of the agencies' human rights abuses in conflict zones such as Aceh, East Timor, and Papua had been viewed in Indonesia as one of the main reasons for Washington's decision to maintain its embargo on all military assistance, a policy the United States put in place after the Indonesian army backed violence that followed East Timor's vote for independence in 1999.[191] Although the alleged murderer, Polycarpus Budi Priyanto, was jailed after the crime, he was acquitted by the Supreme Court in October 2006 for lack of evidence. The case was later reopened by the state prosecutor, who established a link between Priyanto and BIN, despite the latter's denials.[192]

The case remains unsolved and is considered evidence of the Yudhoyono administration's inability to reform its agencies.[193] BIN remains politicized, has successfully reactivated its local networks, and remains capable of conducting the type of black operations carried out under the previous regime. BIN now operates in a much more open, transparent, and pluralistic society—a society that is increasingly intolerant of violations of human and civil rights. This intolerance severely constrains BIN's nuisance capabilities and, although not absolute, is the best guarantee so far against a return to previous undemocratic practices.

## INTELLIGENCE REFORM IN CHILE

Chile represents another interesting case. The center-left coalition elected after the resignation of Augusto Pinochet not only had to disband the infamous National Center for Intelligence (CNI) but also had to reassert control over the military's own intelligence agencies. This happened at a time when the civilian government, operating in a transition framework defined by the military, was still fragile and far from being totally emancipated from military patronage. Because the intelligence agencies had been the favorite instrument of political repression by the previous regime, intelligence reform was a key issue not only for civil-military relations but also for the credibility of the government.

The process that led to a gradual assertion of civilian predominance was, however, a tortuous and difficult one. After years of uneasy relations mixing confrontation and cooperation with the military, the new National Intelligence Agency (ANI) was created in 2004. The new organization did not totally challenge the autonomy of existing military intelligence organizations, however. At the end of the process, the military itself had changed and, although the polarization of the country has not completely disappeared, a return to the situation that prevailed during the dictatorship is no longer possible.

*Civil-military relations and the structure of the Chilean intelligence agencies in Pinochet's Chile.* On September 11, 1973, a military coup d'état ended democracy in Chile, killing the elected president, Salvador Allende, in the process. The following day, the four commanding generals of the armed forces and the police established a military junta. General Augusto Pinochet was designated as president. The new government immediately intended to not only control and neutralize the opposition, which amounted to about 70 percent of the population, but also destroy it.[194] Terror became the rule and arbitrary arrests, torture, and disappearances standard practice.

The creation of the Department of National Intelligence (Dirección de Inteligencia Nacional [DINA]) and the establishment of the state of terror were consubstantial. The clause creating the agency was part of a decree establishing a new institution, the National Prisoners' Service. DINA had the specific task of determining the degree of danger prisoners posed to the state and coordinating with the intelligence services of the armed forces, the police, and the political division of the national detective service. The department quickly became a state within the state.

Even before the 1973 coup, the Chilean military had a prominent role in intelligence and considered intelligence gathering to be "part of its organic role within society, since it believed constant vigilance was critical to maintaining a well-functioning body politic."[195] It had been preceded by a spectacular development in intelligence services in all branches of national defense. As the human and material resources of the services grew, so did their rivalry.[196]

The Ministry of Interior was in charge of the civil police, while each branch of the Ministry of National Defense had its own police force, answerable only to its respective chief of staff. Six autonomous organizations worked with few connections among them. The army, air force, and navy each operated its own agency as well as the Directorate for Public Security and Information and the National Police and Investigations (the investigative arm of the police).[197] The army's Dirección de Inteligencia del Ejército was the group most implicated in spying on civilians.

These forces were autonomous and difficult to control, leading to abuse and political irresponsibility by the state police. By mid-1974, it had become impossible to know the whereabouts of political prisoners and even the cause of their detention. A person detained, interrogated, and released by one police service could be immediately rearrested by another service.[198]

After 1973, intelligence became the most important element of Pinochet's hold on power. He needed, however, to establish control over the intelligence services, which answered only to their own hierarchy and indulged in interservice rivalry at all levels. DINA was created in June 1974. It was a response to the need for a full-scale secret police service under Pinochet's personal command. It was independent of any military structure and tasked with coordinating the work of the other intelligence agencies. DINA put an end to the autonomy of the existing agencies and to the resulting interservice rivalry, and it became the backbone of the regime, the most influential organization at the national level. Personnel for DINA came from all branches of the National Defense

Ministry and also included selected civilians. The army soon became predominant, however. DINA quickly became the main instrument of Pinochet's personal power—Pinochet himself, not the junta, directed intelligence activities.

Retired military officials explain that the creation of DINA was also a way for Pinochet, who was aware of the inevitability of a return to more normal relations between the military and society, to preserve the military institution. As a matter of fact, all three branches of the military involved in the political repression imposed by DINA and later CNI never returned to what can be termed "normal" military activities. Despite acknowledgement of the military's own responsibility in the repression, they insist that DINA was not a military institution.

DINA had five sections: Government Service, Internal, Economics, Psychological Warfare, and External. The two largest divisions, Government Service and Internal, concentrated their efforts on the bureaucracy and on Chilean citizens themselves. Telephones were tapped and mail was opened by the intelligence agencies, which also made arrests and conducted interrogations. The agency ran a network estimated to have employed 20,000 to 30,000 informants, half of whom held strategic positions in government offices throughout Chile. DINA also possessed extraterritorial capabilities that allowed the regime to pursue its opponents outside the country.

DINA was disbanded in August 1977, not because of any sudden concern for human rights but because of strong national and international pressure. A new agency, the CNI, replaced it until the end of the dictatorship. DINA formally depended on the junta, but the CNI was legally linked to the supreme government through the secretary of interior. CNI was, in fact, from the very beginning subordinated to the head of executive power, Augusto Pinochet.[199] One after the other, DINA and the CNI became institutional figures of repression, responsible for torture and murder.

*Political background of the reforms.* The gradual and incomplete assertion of civilian control over the Chilean intelligence agencies cannot be understood without an examination of the evolution of civil-military relations in post-dictatorship Chile. Chile's transition to democracy, which took place under the rules established by the military dictatorship and the resignation of General Pinochet after he was defeated in the October 5, 1988 plebiscite, did not imply an immediate transition from military to civilian rule. As a matter of fact, Chile experienced not one but several transitions that followed different rhythms and time frames. The formal transition ended when General Pinochet handed over power to the newly elected president, Patricio Aylwin, but this did not mark the end of the economic, legal, and social transitions, nor the military one.

Changing the pattern of civil-military relations was a daunting task that required the transformation of the institutional framework to delineate the military's functional autonomy and its institutional involvement in domestic affairs. This was undertaken in a political context characterized by a strong alliance between the right-wing parties and the military. The transition itself had been designed by the outgoing administration. Rejecting opposition calls for a negotiated reform of the 1980 constitution, the Pinochet government unilaterally proposed a set of constitutional changes—in particular, limiting the executive's powers, appointing senators, and reforming the electoral law to favor the right-wing parties—that were ultimately approved with the support of the opposition in a plebiscite in July 1989.[200]

These constitutional changes, especially the electoral law, had an impact not only on the transition itself but also on the very possibility of further changes of the constitution. The conditions existed for a transition—the end of the Cold War and the support of the broader population— but it was severely constrained from the beginning. Subordination of the military had always been an objective of the center-left coalition but, in 1990, the military could remain a quasi-autonomous body because a substantial part of the polity, as expressed through the reformed electoral system, wanted it to retain its autonomy.

Successive presidents used different strategies to deal with the military. Although deprived of the legal tools to reduce military autonomy and lacking a sufficient political majority in the National Congress to introduce the necessary constitutional changes to accomplish this, President Aylwin placed the democratization of Chile's political structures and the goal of national reconciliation at the top of his agenda. He wanted to "reestablish a notion of the armed forces as an essentially obedient, non-deliberative, professional, hierarchical, and disciplined institution."[201] He combined decisiveness with caution. If not confrontational, his strategy was at the very least noncooperative; and he used all legal and political means at his disposal—his veto power over promotions to freeze the careers of officers who had been involved in human rights violations and, more generally, specific gestures, norms of protocol, and symbols—to assert his authority.[202]

Of particular importance was his willingness to demonstrate full political solidarity and support for his government officials in matters closely linked to military affairs. President Aylwin reiterated his confidence in his defense minister, Patricio Rojas, who was pressuring the military by postponing the signing of decrees that regulated internal military matters, whenever the army informally asked for Rojas's resignation.[203] Aylwin's strategy was not without risks as it constantly placed the government in a dilemma: Should it reinforce civilian supremacy or provide political stability? On two occasions, related to a major corruption case in the army, the army resorted to intimidation, once by launching unannounced exercises throughout the country and the second time by declaring a state of alert for five days. The Aylwin administration bypassed such difficulties—and formal institutions such as the National Security Council (NSC) supposedly meant for dealing with national security issues—by developing and cultivating an informal network of military and civilian officials to resolve conflicts.

By contrast, the Eduardo Frei administration that followed the Aylwin administration did seek to promote civilian leadership through cooperation with the military. More business oriented than his predecessor and aware of his own political limitations, Frei focused on the country's modernization rather than change to the political system. He tried to establish a "non-traumatic relationship between the armed forces and some parties of the Concertación [the center-left coalition in power] and particularly, the Christian Democrats."[204] Issues such as constitutional reforms were downplayed. The NSC was no longer bypassed, while President Frei took care to nominate a minister of defense capable of generating confidence in the military.

This strategy failed, however, to prevent the resurgence of a crisis between the government and the military. It created tensions within the ruling coalitions, with some of Frei's partners objecting to his administration's program and gaining a greater say on issues such as human rights and institutional reforms, in turn generating new conflict with the military.

The most significant conflict was on the occasion of the sentencing of Manuel Contreras, former head of DINA and then CNI, to seven years in prison. Contreras had been one of the most reviled figures of the military regime. He and his second in command, Brigadier Pedro Espinoza, were sentenced to prison terms of seven and six years, respectively, by a Chilean court in 1993 for the 1976 assassination of Orlando Letelier in Washington, D.C. Chile's Supreme Court ultimately confirmed the sentence in May 1993 despite repeated attempts at intimidation by Pinochet, who reiterated the warning that he did not know what the reaction of the army would be. Contreras sought refuge in the south of the country; then he was moved with the assistance of the army to a military hospital in central Chile. Finally, both Espinoza and Contreras were jailed, and they completed their sentences despite demonstrations of solidarity by the military.[205]

Manuel Contreras was released in 2001 only to be convicted again in 2002 of masterminding the forced disappearance of Socialist Party leader Victor Olea Alegra, and Contreras was given two life sentences in 2008 for the 1974 murders of General Carlos Prats and his wife in Buenos Aires. The Chilean military did not oppose Contreras's sentences in 2002 or later and did not try to prevent Contreras from being jailed. On the contrary, it dissociated itself from the former head of DINA and CNI. This change in attitude makes apparent the evolution and progress of civil-military relations between the two periods.

A second major source of tension was the debate on the possible impeachment of Augusto Pinochet in 1998. The former dictator was due to retire from the army in March to become a senator for life, according to the 1980 constitution. This placed the government in a difficult situation that was illustrative of the dilemma that all Chilean governments had to face during the period: how to make a significant political gesture, attacking the least democratic aspects of the constitution while respecting the rule of law and avoiding any unconstitutional action. The government, supported by former president Aylwin, opposed impeachment on the grounds that it was detrimental to the transition itself.

The debate took place largely within the ruling coalition, but other moves to change the constitution were opposed by the right, which was closely allied with the military. The National Congress opposed President Frei's proposals to change the composition of the NSC by adding the president of the Chamber of Deputies to upset the balance of power within the

NSC in favor of civilians, abolish appointed senators, and reform the constitutional tribunal. The Frei administration managed, however, to consolidate civilian power through a mix of accommodation and bargaining. If Manuel Contreras ultimately went to jail, the president suspended all action in a famous corruption case known as the "cheque case." He also raised the salaries of the armed forces and reached out to the liberal sectors of the right-wing party on human rights issues, trading the army's demand for closure on the human rights issues for a reduction of the army's prerogatives.

Another factor also deserves particular mention: the progressive reduction of the military budget relative to the overall national gross domestic product during both the Aylwin and Frei presidential terms. Although Aylwin had wanted to reduce the military budget in absolute terms, he had been prevented from doing so by his lack of a two-thirds majority in both houses of Congress. He then had to follow the law, which stipulated that the military budget had to be the same as the budget had been in 1989 except for adjustments for annual inflation. As a result of the growth of the Chilean economy, the military budget significantly declined in relative terms—a trend that continued under Frei—from 2.96 percent in 1989 (17.20 percent of the national budget) to 1.56 percent in 1997 (8.94 percent of the national budget). As a consequence, the legitimacy of successive civilian governments increased as the military budget declined.

At the end of Frei's term, civil-military relations had reached a modus vivendi. The military could no longer block all government policies, even when they affected major military interests. The military respected court decisions, although together with its civilian allies it sought ad hoc measures to mitigate the rulings' effects. As observed by Gregory Weeks: "The key to civil-military stability was refraining from criticizing the armed forces, attempting gradual reforms, and fostering a better technical and more apolitical relationship with the Defense Ministry."[206]

The presidential victory of Ricardo Lagos in January 2000 did not change the trend. Although he was the first socialist since Salvador Allende to be elected president, he immediately demonstrated his willingness to establish a solid working relationship with the military by nominating a defense minister, Mario Fernandez, whom the military trusted. From the perspective of civil-military relations, Lagos's presidency was the continuation of those of his Christian Democratic predecessors.

The defining event for the evolution of civil-military relations took place in Chile across two presidencies—the arrest of Augusto Pinochet in London in 1998. The arrest further stimulated military subordination to the civilian democratic authorities. Both the Frei and Lagos administrations mobilized their diplomatic resources to prevent the extradition of the former dictator to Spain, where he was charged by Judge Baltasar Garzon for torture and conspiracy to commit torture. The arrest inevitably provoked political tensions but did not result in a renewed civilmilitary crisis; on the contrary, it displayed relative national unity.[207] The military institution expressed its solidarity with its former commander in chief but maintained a subordinate attitude toward President Frei. It complied with requests to provide new information on the disappearances of political dissidents during the dictatorship as part of the "dialogue roundtable" initiated by President Frei, which included the participation of the military, victims, and civil society representatives.

But the Chilean judicial system continued its work in parallel. A number of Chilean judges increased their efforts to bring military officials guilty of atrocities to court to face charges of murder, kidnapping, and torture. Pinochet was soon stripped of his immunity and the Supreme Court reinterpreted the 1978 amnesty, stating that the amnesty could be applied only to persons, not institutions, but only after an investigation had been carried out and a judicial decision had been reached. The decision affected not only Pinochet but also many other officers. By January 2002, more than a hundred retired officers had been charged for known deaths and disappearances.[208]

This slow but continuous work of the judicial process is one of the defining characteristics of the Chilean transition toward democracy. Although Eduardo Frei was, at times, tempted to address the problem of human rights violations as a political instrument to deal with the military, successive civilian governments have tried to avoid that trap and have shifted the problem where it belongs—to the judiciary. Although difficult and at times dangerous, using the judicial process did help establish solidly civilian supremacy over the long term. The military ultimately officially endorsed the democratic system and rejected human rights abuse as an instrument of power.

At the end of the Lagos presidency in 2006, the two radically opposite views of civil-military relations that had been contradicting each other in Chile since

1990 were gradually reconciled. The armed forces had long maintained that civil-military relations were still to be governed by the 1980 constitution and the legal and practical changes introduced in 1989 at the end of the military government. All civilian governments, in contrast, had worked to restore civilian supremacy over the armed forces in accordance with the pre-1973 constitutional and customary principles.[209] The polarization of society, on the one hand, and the polarization of civil military relations, on the other, persisted. It took time before Pinochet finally resigned from his senate post.

The civil-military relationship emerged relatively unscathed at the end of the Lagos era, during which General Cheyre, commander in chief of the army, acknowledged in a 2003 speech the institutional responsibility for past wrongdoing and announced that the army was "on the way to adjusting to the principles and values of democracy as a political system and respect for human dignity as the vital element for a sound national and international coexistence."[210] Ultimately, Lagos's presidency was marked by the adoption of a new set of constitutional reforms that drastically restricted military autonomy. The election of Michelle Bachelet in 2006—herself the daughter of an air force general and member of Allende's cabinet who had been arrested after the 1973 coup and who had died in prison after being tortured—marked the beginning of a new era. Chilean armed forces are still able to exert various pressures on civilian. In practice, this meant controlling labor organization policy makers, but there is no longer the threat of a rebellion or a coup d'état. The Chilean military, to a large extent, has returned to its tradition of professionalism, legalism, and constitutionalism.

*Process of reforming intelligence agencies.* Debates over the reform of the intelligence agencies and the reforms themselves reflect the evolution of Chile's political system, illustrating the constant tension between civilians and the military and reflecting the gradual change in the balance of power between the two. More important, they also demonstrate the long and difficult process of confidence building.

Reforming intelligence had always been part of the center-left coalition agenda. The objective has been to centralize intelligence in an institution controlled by the president and put an end to a situation in which each branch of the military has had its own intelligence service accountable only to the commander in chief. Yet nothing could really be done during the four years immediately following the reestablishment of democracy. The total mistrust between civilians and the army and the willingness of the army to demonstrate that democrats were not able to control society and deliver on security prevented all serious cooperation between the two.

The situation was understandable given recent history but paradoxical because the main threat the new regime was actually facing was not coming from the right-wing parties allied to the military but from the far left. The terrorism emanating from groups such as Movimiento de la Izquierda Revolucionaria, Lautaro, and the Frente Patriótica Manuel Rodríguez was a greater problem for Chile's young and fragile democracy than the military, which had agreed to the transition. The same groups that had fought the dictatorship were now a problem for the nascent democracy and had to be eliminated although through different means than those used by DINA and the

CNI. Former employees of the CNI, disbanded after the resignation of Pinochet, were also seen as potentially dangerous, but the threat never really materialized. Some members later joined organized crime syndicates, but they never reconstituted a politico-military force able to challenge the government.

***Department for Public Security and Intelligence.*** Reforming the agencies in a situation in which civilians received no information from a totally uncooperative military was very difficult but necessary. The dissolution of CNI after the resignation of Pinochet from his position as commander in chief of the military had created an organizational vacuum. Political repression had stopped but coordination mechanisms had disappeared in the process, leaving each agency to return to its previous autonomy and, to some extent, the civilian-military standoff. Moreover, the new civilian governments had no previous experience in intelligence work. Before they could embark on intelligence reform, they faced significant obstacles in dismantling structures the military considered central to the nation's protection, and they were also deprived of any effective intelligence instrument by the uncooperative military.

Intelligence cooperation had to be built before it could be institutionalized. This was done gradually through the Ministry of Defense and the Ministry of Interior and involved meetings in which government officials and the heads of intelligence of the army, air force, navy, and police took part. Bilateral meetings and personal contacts also happened more frequently. A division of labor naturally occurred, with the police producing intelligence on domestic affairs, including ordinary criminality and activism of the far left, while the army was concerned with external intelligence, although it kept an eye on the domestic political process and the agents of political mobilization within the country.

The institutionalization of the process was both symbolic—given the role of intelligence during the dictatorship—and operational as an integral part of the assertion of civilian preeminence. At the same time, the new institutions could be meaningful only if they reflected the actual balance of power between civilians and the military within the country. Therefore, if the law that created the Department for Public Security and Intelligence (Dirección de Seguridad Pública e Informaciones [DSPI]) in 1993 was the first real attempt to control intelligence in Chile, it was a limited one.

The DSPI depended on the Ministry of Interior to be in charge of coordinating the activities of domestic public security. Its function was to "provide the information, studies, analysis and assessment of intelligence required for the government to formulate policies and adopt specific measures and actions with respect to terrorist actions and conduct"[211] as well as crime and threats to public order. In this context, the role of the new agency was essentially a coordinating one. Through the Ministry of Defense, its role was to obtain information from the intelligence organs of the armed forces and to provide the government with the analysis and planning necessary for the conduct of its policy. It was also tasked with coordinating the exchange of information between the public agencies in charge of gathering intelligence and providing the public agencies with the domestic information entering the scope of their own responsibilities.[212] The

Consultative Intelligence Committee was created for this purpose. It was composed of an under secretary of the Ministry of Defense, the deputy chief of staff of the Ministry of Defense, the under secretary for external relations, the director of public security and information, the heads of intelligence of each branch of the armed forces, and the heads of intelligence of the public security institutions. The committee was chaired by the under secretary of the interior.[213]

The new institution had no independent means of collecting intelligence and was entirely dependent on the goodwill of the intelligence branches of the armed forces and police. Its efficiency and relevance were therefore entirely the result of the good or bad personal relations entertained by the various protagonists, and the military linked its cooperation to the position of the government on the question of past human rights violations. The suspicion toward civilian power remained high, and several cases of government officials' being spied on were reported during the 1990s. The police, however, played a more positive role than the military and proved to be more cooperative.

The civilian government was aware of the weaknesses of the new intelligence mechanism, but it was prevented from acting more decisively by the links between the military and the parliamentary right, as the electoral system gave the military parliamentary representation that was far above its actual electoral weight. The military could therefore continue acting indirectly through its political allies. In 1995, a proposal by President Frei to centralize intelligence and establish more civilian control was defeated in Parliament before it could even be debated.[214]

*Creation of the National Intelligence Agency (ANI).* It was no surprise that during the presidency of Ricardo Lagos a new reform of the intelligence system took place. The relationship between civilians and the military had, by then, built sufficient confidence to allow a new step. The process that led to the creation of the new institution was, however, another example of the unease in civilian-military relations.

The Chilean Congress started debating the creation of ANI as early as 2001. It soon became clear that the autonomy of the existing military and other existing intelligence agercies would not be challenged. As the new agency did not affect any of the military's prerogatives, the military did not oppose its creation.

The debate between civilian and military elements focused essentially on the scope of the mandate of the agency. Concerned with antiterrorism, the military wanted the mandate to be as broad as possible. It initially supported the creation of ANI and lost interest when it perceived the new agency would be too weak to fulfill what was to be its main mission, counterterrorism. By contrast, the civilian branch, the left in particular, was concerned about internal surveillance, while the government wanted to limit the scope of the agency.

ANI's creation was finally approved by the Senate in May 2003 and final legislation was passed in October 2004. The law that created ANI stated in Article 20 that "the conduct of military intelligence services corresponds to the appropriate military institution to which they belong," their objectives being set by their respective commander in chief.[215] Similarly, the internal controls remained under the supervision of the heads of the agencies, who in fact define the role of their organizations.[216]

The differences between ANI and its predecessor organization were important. The law of 2004 stated that if the Intelligence Committee was composed of the heads of other intelligence agencies and had a coordinating function, the existing intelligence agencies were now required by law to provide ANI with the requested intelligence. Although such provisions are always difficult to implement in practice because the various agencies could always pretend that they did not possess the information they were requested to provide, the decision to cooperate was in theory no longer solely the prerogative of the military.

Even more significant was the fact that the new agency was no longer confined to a coordinating role but was also responsible for collecting intelligence.[217] In practice it still relied on intelligence provided by the intelligence agencies of the armed forces, but it also had independent intelligence- gathering capabilities that, among other things, allowed it to verify information, although the law still left a considerable degree of autonomy to the agencies. ANI was, for example, provided with the power to enact measures against narcotics trafficking and terrorism. Activities involving "national security," such as tapping telephones and surveillance of the electronic media, were left to the intelligence services of the armed forces. Permission had to be requested but could be granted by a military judge.[218]

Of particular importance also was the fact that ANI was responsible not only to the Ministry of Interior but also, through the ministry, to the president himself, who appointed the director of the agency.[219]

An intelligence committee was created in the lower house of the legislature, but the actual control exercised over the intelligence agencies is difficult to assess, given the secrecy of their activities. Some observers consider that Chile's military intelligence agencies have been left to themselves. [220] The creation of an ANI that did not bring individual military agencies under civilian control could also have raised some suspicion that it might again be used as an instrument of repression by the power of the day. Whatever the reality of this assertion, the existence of parliamentary oversight, even if symbolic, is an integral component of the assertion of civilian predominance over the military.

As a result, if the creation of a civilian agency is considered in isolation, it is not clear whether it in fact advanced civilian supremacy over the armed forces. The highly autonomous intelligence agencies created by the military regime continue to elude civilian oversight. This is considered a failure by some observers, given the successes of the Senate in increasing civilian power over commanders in chief and the elimination of designated senators. In the field of intelligence, however, the Senate seems to have been unable to totally overcome the resistance of the military, revealing a lack of consistency as well as the absence of a clearly defined policy visà- vis the military.

The creation of ANI should, however, be considered in a larger perspective. There is no doubt that the creation of ANI was an imperfect attempt at democratic control of intelligence agencies in Chile. It was, however, an essential and necessary step in the assertion of civilian power. ANI was the result of the evolution of military-civilian relations in favor of civilian authority and, to some extent, it helped to create the conditions for further evolution. Despite the imperfections of the system, a return to the abuses of DINA and CNI is now unthinkable, as are the prospects of a new coup d'état in Chile. The political polarization of the country may persist, yet the peaceful transition toward a more transparent system and the acceptance by the military of the rules of the democratic game are undoubtedly models to be sought in Pakistan and elsewhere. Chile's military was not a loser in the process: it gradually regained its popularity as it accepted its own depoliticization.

## LESSONS FROM THE CHILEAN AND INDONESIAN CASES

Because all democratic transitions are different, the process by which a new democratic government establishes control over its intelligence agencies is unique and depends on a number of specific variables. It would be futile to compare the experiences of different countries too narrowly, regardless of their successes or failures. Some lessons for Pakistan can nevertheless be drawn from the Chilean and Indonesian experiences.

*Establishing democratic control over intelligence agencies is a long-term process.* It took, for example, fourteen years before Chile could pass a law establishing a civilian agency, ANI, with real, although limited, power over its military counterparts.

The main characteristic of the Chilean case is that the institutionalization of democratic control over the intelligence agencies follows very closely the evolution of the political balance of power between civilian institutions and the military. Intelligence agency reform reflects the evolution of the polity as a whole. Indonesia, by contrast, has institutionalized the control of its intelligence agencies much faster than it established the predominance of civilians. As a result, control is formal but not always effective.

Time is therefore an important component of the sustainability of any reform process, not least because it takes time for mentalities to evolve. The change of generations in military leadership is an integral component of democratic evolution.

*Reforms of the institutions must be consistent with the reality of the political system.* A distinction also has to be made between the democratic process and the reality of the balance of power between the civilian and military realms. The degree of institutionalization of the control system of the intelligence agencies is not an absolute indicator of the extent of this control.

The democratic process—of which the control of the intelligence agencies is a part—should be a permanent effort. There should, however, always be a relative consistency between the level of institutionalization and the control of the intelligence agencies.

This may imply pauses in the reform process as well as temporarily incomplete or unsatisfactory control. A significant gap between the law and the reality can be counterproductive, as it can be used by the agencies as a pretext to oppose necessary changes.

*The military must cooperate.* No democratization process has taken place without the consent and participation of the military. Consequently, no control of the intelligence agencies has ever been established without the military's cooperation or at least assent. It is only when he understood that he no longer had the support of the military—some of his generals had urged him to resign—that Suharto stepped down. Similarly, in Chile, the transition toward democracy had been prepared by the military itself. The mechanism the officers established was biased in their own favor as they introduced constitutional amendments and distorted the electoral process to give the right wing power much greater than its actual electoral weight. Nevertheless, they respected the process set in place and established the framework in which reform of the intelligence agencies took place. Even if they did not initially cooperate, they did not sabotage the process. Their resistance was, moreover, linked to concern over accountability for involvement in political repression more than to principled opposition of a certain degree of political control. The process itself consisted of building a confident relationship with the military.

*Civil society and public opinion must play roles in the reforms.* The role of civil society is an essential, yet complex element of establishing democratic control over intelligence agencies. In both Indonesia and Chile, the population's intolerance of security establishment abuses has been a defining factor in the democratic transition and the dismantling of the most repressive state institutions. In Indonesia, civil society and public opinion constitute the best guarantee that there will be no return to the situation that prevailed during the dictatorship.

In both countries the success of the civilian governments in establishing their predominance over the militaries and their agencies can partly be explained by their capacity to temper the expectations of civil society and larger opinion. This careful management gave them the necessary room for maneuver with their militaries and allowed the compromises necessary for the creation of working relationships that later developed into confidence building.

This was particularly obvious in the case of Chile, where the civilian government always operated between two major constraints: the demands for justice from a substantial part of the population and the government's weakness vis-à-vis the military agencies that it did not control. The policy of not using as a political instrument the human rights violations committed by the agencies during the dictatorship and, instead, transferring them to the judiciary allowed the government to maintain public pressure and constrain the military, but this policy also gave the government and the military the capacity to compromise by individualizing the process. The army had long rejected its own officers guilty of atrocities in DINA and later the CNI. By the time the army chief of staff, General Juan Emilio Cheyre, publicly acknowledged the responsibility of the army for some of the abuses, the institution had gradually lost much of its power through the process. The military institution could then cooperate fully again with a civilian government whose predominance it had accepted.

A cautious use of symbolism in this context was useful for managing public expectations. The Aylwin government, for example, always put forward symbols of civilian supremacy without humiliating the military, and at the same time it never gave up its willingness to bring to trial the major human rights violators during the repression.

Civilian indifference after major violations as in the past can also be a problem. In Indonesia, for example, the lack of motivation on the part of civilians for intelligence reforms has prevented successive civilian governments from establishing as much control over the agencies as the political balance of power would have allowed. Other fields of the democratization process proceeded more quickly and more successfully.

*The international context is of vital importance.* The international context is also a central factor in any democratic transition and, therefore, in the democratic control of the intelligence agencies. It can, however, influence the process positively and negatively. Even though the national situations were decisive in the coups d'état of both Suharto and Pinochet, there is no doubt that the Cold War context greatly facilitated the projects of the aspiring dictators. Their respective endeavors were at the very least tolerated by the international community, and in the case of Chile were helped by the United States with little concern for the methods employed. Similarly, between 500,000 and 800,000 people were massacred in Indonesia in the name of anticommunism without much international protest. Although comparable in scope, the abuses of the Chilean regime have been well documented since the end of the Pinochet regime in 1990. It should be acknowledged that the progressive change of position of U.S. administrations was initiated by an operation conducted as early as September 1976 on U.S. soil by Chilean intelligence agencies—the murder in Washington, D.C., of Orlando Letelier, a former minister in the Allende government.

In turn, the end of the Cold War greatly facilitated the acceptance of regime change in both Indonesia and Chile. As the communist threat disappeared, right-wing dictators were no longer necessary. Human rights and democracy therefore became the order of the day and the use of intelligence agencies as instruments of political repression insufferable.

CHAPTER

# 6

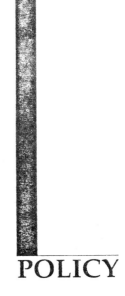

# POLICY
# RECOMMENDATIONS

Because of the importance of Pakistan to the issue of terrorism, the community of nations, including Pakistan itself, is vitally concerned about the role of the intelligence agencies in Pakistan. The main obstacle the international community is confronted with, however, is of a psychological nature, the belief that the supremacy of the intelligence agencies in Pakistan is a fact of life and that nothing can be done about it. The examples of Indonesia and Chile demonstrate the contrary, even though change comes at a cost.

## ROLE OF THE INTERNATIONAL COMMUNITY

From the perspective of the international community, the issue of democratic control of Pakistan's intelligence agencies is primarily the consequence of its concern with international terrorism. Western countries can be either a facilitating or an inhibiting factor, but they will be affected by the outcome of the process through the persistence or disappearance of terrorism emanating from the tribal areas along the Afghan–Pakistan border.

Most Western governments are reluctant to aid such a process, even passively. They believe that ending cooperation with the ISI would simply increase the terrorist threat on their national territories. For several reasons, this perception should be questioned:

- The threat of terrorism will persist as long as the ISI continues nurturing a number of extremist groups operating within and beyond Pakistan's borders. Therefore, compromises with Pakistan's main intelligence agency buy additional security only marginally and create a rent for the ISI. Besides creating an additional problem for the elected government, deals with the ISI perpetuate the ISI's dominance. As the ISI's control over terrorist groups diminishes, the rationale for the rent (the need for cooperation and the subsequent compromises) diminishes, too, although it does not totally disappear.

- The end of ISI interference would not automatically mean the end of terrorism and the insurgency in the tribal belt, but it would allow for real cooperation with Pakistani intelligence to take place.

- Given the likelihood of retaliation should any of these groups conduct a major terrorist operation on U.S.

soil, the constraint is as much a reality for the ISI and its military patrons as for the ISI's Western partners.

- The control of the intelligence agencies is a component of civil-military relations. The ISI is a military body, and the operational responsibility to control it belongs to the military and its leadership. International policies intended to restrain the role of the Pakistani intelligence agencies will have to ensure that they do not weaken the civilian government in the process, a situation that would ultimately be counterproductive.

Any arm-twisting measures or mechanisms will have to be looked for between this set of constraints and structural factors, considering the risk for the West but also the Pakistani security establishment's objectives. International actors with an interest in Pakistan's situation should aim for the long term, taking into account current Pakistani vulnerabilities.

*Work through the Pakistan government.* Most of the countries involved in the region are now aware of the double-dealing of the ISI and are asking the Pakistan government to better control its intelligence apparatus. The problem is that the same Western governments that today blame the Pakistani state for its inability to control its agencies are maintaining working relations with these very same agencies, thus undermining their own purpose and the credibility of the Pakistan government as well as its legitimacy. This situation diminishes the Pakistan government's leverage to take control of the intelligence agencies. The ISI is, in turn, vindicated.

*Mobilize all of the countries with some degree of influence on the Pakistan military.* Because China is itself a victim of Islamist terrorism, it is a potential partner whose influence on the Pakistan military is far greater than any Western country. Beijing may still be reluctant to cooperate with Western countries, but China is likely to become a target of extremism owing, for example, to its role in the Red Mosque incident, during which Beijing convinced former president Musharraf to intervene militarily.

*Condition all assistance to the Pakistan military on actual results, not only in the fight against terrorism but in controlling its intelligence agencies.* Experience has shown that Pakistan can hand over international terrorists as a way of achieving restraint from the West in demands regarding the Taliban. Concentrating exclusively on this kind of result is at best insufficiently effective, hence the need to concentrate on the structures and institutions that actually support terrorism.

One may argue that the resistance may be strong and the risk of retaliation real if the Pakistan government cooperates in the fight against terrorism. The argument has validity but is gradually weakening as the Pakistani intelligence agencies seem to have lost control of some of the groups they initially supported. More important, however, is that Pakistan's security forces are themselves victims of terrorism. This convergence of interests should be emphasized through technical assistance whenever cooperation is sincere and unbiased but should leave no room for compromise with regard to the terrorist organizations targeted by Pakistan's security apparatus and to the need to place intelligence agencies under authoritative civilian control.

*Diminish the importance of Pakistan for the international community's engagement in Afghanistan.*

Pakistan is currently in the unique position of supporting both sides in the Afghan conflict, whereas the international community is inhibited in its relations with Islamabad because Pakistan was until recently the only country of transit for support and supplies for the international troops in Afghanistan. The opening of a Russian route has not solved this problem as the International Security Assistance Force (ISAF) remains dependent on its relations with Moscow, which are at the mercy of issues external to Afghanistan but extremely important for almost all the actors in Afghanistan. There is, in fact, no ideal situation as almost all the regional actors have some problems with the NATO component of the coalition. The solution can therefore come only from more countries' accepting transit of ISAF supplies through their territory. These could include China and Iran, because both countries have at least partially convergent interests with ISAF in the area. Islamabad's leverage would thus be greatly diminished and the room for maneuver of the international community increased.

These actions would help to gradually reverse the link of dependency between the international community and Pakistan without violating Islamabad's sovereignty. They could also help reinforce civilian predominance.

## RECOMMENDATIONS TO THE GOVERNMENT OF PAKISTAN

Pakistan's intelligence agencies cannot be reformed in isolation. Because the Pakistani intelligence agencies, the MI and ISI, are part of the military, a policy aiming at establishing civilian control over these agencies is only part of the larger design of asserting civilian predominance. Several of the recommendations listed below would apply equally to this more general objective. They are also relevant to the specific issues at stake. Some are more concerned with the intelligence agencies. None of the recommendations is decisive if taken individually. All concentrate on a more transparent system and, therefore, more accountability.

***Strengthen and develop the police.*** In the short and medium term, the Pakistan government will have no choice but to cooperate with the existing intelligence agencies. This should not prevent the government from maximizing the separation between the agencies and giving each of them its due role and corresponding means.

The two processes are closely linked. Problems facing the armed forces, the police, and the intelligence agencies are interconnected. The weakness of one of these institutions tends to reinforce the extension of the others beyond their expected roles. As observed by Felipe Agüero: "A weak or ineffective police will put pressure on officials to use the military in policing roles for which it is ill prepared, or to militarize the police. The existence of several poorly controlled intelligence agencies may harm the professionalism of military and police."[221]

In both Chile and Indonesia, strengthening the police was integral to the reassertion of civilian control over the intelligence agencies, although with different degrees of success. The police in Indonesia are seen as a corrupt, inefficient institution, whereas the perception in Chile is the opposite.

In Pakistan, the domestic extension of the ISI presence (down to the district level) has been the reverse of the weakening of the police. Diminishing the ISI's domestic role will therefore require the strengthening of the police in parallel with the redefinition of the ISI's role, which should no longer interfere in domestic affairs.

The police force is known for its corruption, politicization, and basic inability to perform its duty of protecting citizens against crime and violence. Its reform will therefore be a prerequisite for a more balanced relationship among the intelligence agencies. According to the International Crisis Group, the police are also not immune from penetration by sectarian and jihadist elements as a result of deliberate state policies,[222] but the police resent the Musharraf government for its neglect of the police force. Reforming the police would therefore be a difficult endeavour but a promising one, as this resentment would most certainly benefit any government willing to help the institution fulfill the role—implementing law and order— that should normally belong to it.

The question of police capabilities remains a major issue that could be greatly eased by international assistance. The international community has ultimately everything to gain in the strengthening of the police, as it would be a much more effective counterterrorism mechanism if trained and equipped properly. As the International Crisis Group recently recommended: helping the police "with training and technical assistance would pay counter-terrorism dividends."[223] Such aid would be of great help in establishing the credibility of Pakistan's new government both domestically and internationally, creating the basis for a more confident relationship with the military as well.

*Reinforce the separation between military and civilian intelligence agencies.* To be effective, the reform should not stop at the police. The incestuous relationship between the ISI and the IB should be stopped, and the possibility of ISI agents' moving into civilian bodies should be controlled and limited. The ISI's ability to gain influence in the NAB by providing funding in exchange for the recruitment of former ISI agents is a good example of how one agency can gradually develop influence over another. Such cross-recruitment should be stopped if the organizations are to become independent.

*Civilianize the debate on foreign and security policies.* No democratic control of the intelligence agencies will be possible without a prior reappropriation by the Pakistani polity of the public debate on Pakistan's foreign and security policies. Only such a debate can help stablish a consensus on the objectives and thus provide a framework for the agencies' own task. The agencies' actions would no longer be left only to their own initiative nor to the sole decision of the military. Moreover, public debate and civilian policy formulation would provide a reference point against which the actions or nonactions of the agencies could be assessed.

What is essential in the process is the delegitimation of the political role of the intelligence agencies and the redefinition of their role in conformity with the national interests of the country, as decided by the newly elected government and approved by Parliament as the expression of the nation's common political will.[224] The absence of consensus on foreign and security policies would make the problem intractable. When confronted with international accusations of ISI responsibility in the recent terrorist attack against the Indian embassy in Kabul, President Musharraf and the COAS, General Kayani, playing once again on the nationalist feelings of the population, promptly denounced the accusations as a conspiracy against the ISI and the Pakistan military that supposedly endangered Pakistani security. It is therefore essential to adopt a common definition of the national interest. This redefinition will allow a clearer separation of what, in the Pakistani context, is patriotic or unpatriotic.

The reappropriation of the debate on foreign and security policies is the primary responsibility of Pakistan's Parliament. It would undoubtedly be difficult to prevent the political parties from playing emotional cards in a context where the traditional—in particular, religious—identity issue is likely to confuse the debate, but such a debate is essential. Civil society and public opinion more generally should also be involved through the press.

*Stand up to the military whenever necessary.* A fine line will inevitably have to be drawn between unnecessarily confronting the military and the need to stand up to it whenever constitutional order requires.

Although the director general of ISI is theoretically nominated by and accountable to the prime minister, the director general is in fact accountable primarily to the COAS. Every attempt by civilian prime ministers thus far to nominate an ISI director general of their own liking, without the consent of the military, has ended in failure; this illustrates the fact that legality is often at odds with reality in Pakistan.

There can be no soft substitute for the fact that the director general of the ISI is legally accountable primarily to the prime minister and not to the COAS. This does not and should not prevent discussions and the reaching of a consensus before the nomination itself takes place. Once decided, however, the director general is constitutionally accountable to the prime minister and no one else. One may argue that examples presented in these pages show that this is wishful thinking; however, two points about this need to be made.

First, it is unclear whether, after eight years of Musharraf's rule, the military is ready for yet another coup. The decision of the COAS, Parvez Kayani, to maintain relative neutrality during the February 2008 elections was understood by many in the military as necessary for restoring the prestige and professionalism of the army. It was preferable to let the civilians bear the burden of day-to-day government and reap the unpopularity inevitably associated with it.

Second, since the 2008 elections, the ISI seems to have launched a series of offensives both on the Afghan border and in Kashmir, which, besides their specific geostrategic objectives, also create a credibility problem for the civilian government.

This raises a number of questions regarding the real position of the Pakistan military. If it seems unlikely that it again wants to assume direct control, it also seems clear that the military intends to signal that it is still a force to reckon with. If compelled to clarify its position, the military could find itself faced with a dilemma between its willingness to adopt a low profile and protecting the ISI as the executor of the military's dirty work, a position it may find uncomfortable. The current situation favors the military only as long as the civilians refuse to confront it, but this could turn in favor of civilians if a confrontation arises.

*Restore the Supreme Court and bring ISI's violations of legality to the court.* Nowhere, except in a dictatorship, do intelligence agencies operate outside a legal framework. Such a framework exists in Pakistan but is ignored by the institutions concerned. It is therefore a necessary part of the democratization process to bring the intelligence agencies' violations before the courts to reestablish the preeminence of the judiciary, not out of revenge, but to assert civilian power. It is also essential to avoid using forgiveness for past abuses as an asset for a political bargain with regard to the control of the intelligence agencies. The natural judicial instance for such a matter would be Pakistan's Supreme Court, which is at the origin of the current political crisis and whose fate is not yet sealed. In the short term, this situation is in obvious contradiction with the necessity to depoliticize the process as much as possible. But the establishment of the rule flaw is a prerequisite not only for the demilitarization of Pakistan's political life but also for obtaining control of the agencies.

It could be argued that the weakness of the current judiciary will inevitably be another obstacle to establishing such control. The Chilean example demonstrates that similar difficulties can be overcome and that it is essential not to bargain the political control of the agencies against any form of amnesty that would leave the agencies' legal violations unpunished.

Judicial control does not contradict the nature of intelligence agencies and the secrecy of their activities. Control should be over the purpose, reach, and objects of the agencies' work, not about how they do their job under the law.

*Manage public expectations.* The careful management of public expectations is ultimately an important factor of failure or success. The difficulty stems partly from the fact that, coming after years of military rule during which the practices of the intelligence agencies were at once an open secret and a taboo, nobody really dares to confront the agencies.

Opening a debate about the control of the intelligence agencies could raise popular expectations beyond reasonable objectives. Yet no reform of the system will be possible without mobilizing the population. Whatever the country, the primary driver of intelligence reform in relation to domestic political affairs has always been the intolerance of the population. This intolerance is often the best guarantee against a return to previous practices after reform has taken place. The press undoubtedly must play a central role in keeping intelligence agencies in the public eye.

At the same time, however, no reform of the intelligence agencies in general or simply of the ISI will be possible without the cooperation of the military. To achieve both the objective of reform and the cooperation of the military, the reform itself will have to be discussed with the military and the military's role recognized within the limits of the consensus produced by an eventual public debate on foreign policy.

# CONCLUSION

Pakistan is only at the very beginning of a process whose success is still uncertain. Patience will be necessary, for both the Pakistan government and the international community. Both face a similar dilemma: terrorism is an urgent threat that intelligence institutions must combat, but civilians need to assert their supremacy and control over these institutions. Any attempt by the Pakistan government to enforce control prematurely is likely to end in disaster.

Yet, patience should not be an alibi for inaction. Pakistan's civilian government would be wrong to ignore the need to decisively establish its supremacy over the intelligence community. Reducing the role of the military in intelligence should be a priority not only because it will help the government consolidate itself domestically but also because the perception abroad of Pakistan's emerging democracy and consequent foreign support will be shaped by its capacity to impose its authority on the intelligence agencies' activities on issues ranging from domestic terrorism to foreign policy.

Change is never easy, and redirecting intelligence agencies to uphold a democratic dispensation is a real challenge. Although every transition is unique and the experiences of Indonesia and Chile are not wholly applicable to Pakistan, lessons can be learned from their experiences.

First, change is possible even in countries where not so long ago military regimes were stronger and more brutal than the one in Pakistan. Asserting civilian control over the intelligence agencies in Indonesia and Chile has brought about different results, reflecting the various characteristics of the democratization process, but the reassertion of civilian control over the militaries of Indonesia and Chile has nevertheless been a reality.

Second, change is always slow, frustrating, and painful. During the early days of any reform, the new intelligence services are essentially the same as the old ones. It is only over time that the old apparatus can change significantly. The depth of the change is always a direct function of the depth of the democratization process. Civilian mobilization, or, on the contrary, indifference, is a central factor. Democratic control of the intelligence agencies is not the prerogative of a few specialists in the fields— Chilean democrats coming to power in 1990 had no previous experience with intelligence work—nor should it be limited to them. Before being translated into institutions, control begins with the population's intolerance of a repressive apparatus.

A last conclusion should be drawn by Pakistan from the Indonesian and, more important, the Chilean experiences. Intelligence reform per se is not automatically beneficial to democratic civil-military relations. Taking absolute control out the hands of the military and placing it into the hands of one president or prime minister constitutes neither a guarantee against civilian authoritarianism nor a guarantee of democratic progress. Establishing legal guidelines for effective parliamentary oversight must be part of the overall process. Ultimately, what is at stake is the balance of power that will eventually emerge in the new system. The control of the intelligence agencies can be, at best, only as democratic as the system in which it takes place.

## ENDNOTES

1   Iftikhar H. Malik, State and Civil Society in Pakistan: Politics of Authority, Ideology, and Ethnicity (New York: St. Martin's Press, 1997), p. 104.

2   Hassan Abbas, "Reform of Pakistan's Intelligence Services," Watandost, March 15, 2008, <http://watandost. blogspot. com/2008/03/reform-ofpakistans- intelligence.html>.

3   Mohajirs are migrants from India.

4   "White Paper on Intelligence," South African Government Information, 1995,

&lt;www.intelligence.gov.za/Legislation/white_paper_on_intelligence. htm&gt;.

5    Hans Born and Ian Leigh, Making Intelligence Accountable: Legal Standards and Best Practice for Oversight of Intelligence Agencies (Oslo: Geneva Center for the Democratic Control of Armed Forces/ Publishing House of the Parliament of Norway, 2005), p. 13.

6    Gregory Weeks, "A Preference for Deference: Reforming the Military's Intelligence Role in Argentina, Chile and Peru," Third World Quarterly, vol. 29, no. 1 (2008), p. 48.

7    Ibid.

8    Richard Tanter, "East Timor and the Crisis of the Indonesian Intelligence State," in Richard Tanter, Mark Selden, and Stephen L. Shalom, eds., Bitter Flowers, Sweet Flowers: East Timor, Indonesia and the World Community (Lanham, Md.: Rowman & Littlefield, 2001), p. 197.

9    Angel Rabasa and John Haseman, eds., The Military and Democracy in Indonesia: Challenges, Politics and Power (Santa Monica, Calif.: Rand Corporation, 2002), p. 2.

10   Muthiah Alagappa, Coercion and Governance: The Declining Political Role of the Military in Asia (Stanford: Stanford University Press, 2001), p. 2.

11   Hasan-Askari Rizvi, "Civil-Military Relations in Contemporary, Pakistan," Survival, vol. 40, no. 2 (Summer 1998), p. 96.

12   Ibid.

13   Ibid., p. 100.

14   Ibid.

15   "Directorate for Inter-Services Intelligence [ISI]," Federation of American Scientists (FAS), Intelligence Resource Program, July 25, 2002, &lt;www.fas. org/irp/world/pakistan/isi/index.html&gt;.

16 "Directorate for Inter-Services Intelligence [ISI]," Global Security.org, April 26, 2005, <www.globalsecurity.org//intell/world/pakistan/isi.htm>.

17 The Joint Intelligence Bureau is also popularly known as the "political wing" or "political cell."

18 "Directorate for Inter-Services Intelligence [ISI]," FAS.

19 Altaf Gauhar, "How Intelligence Agencies Run Our Politics," *Nation*, August 17, 1997, p. 4.

20 Since the late 1990s, MI is also represented in each district.

21 Sean P. Winchell, "Pakistan's ISI: The Invisible Government," International Journal of Intelligence and CounterIntelligence, vol. 16, no. 3 (Fall 2003), p. 375.

22 Ibid.

23 Ibid.

24 Gauhar, "How Intelligence Agencies Run Our Politics," p. 4.

25 Ibid.

26 Ibid.

27 Malik, State and Civil Society in Pakistan, p. 95.

28 Hasan-Askari Rizvi, Military, State and Society in Pakistan (New York: St. Martin's Press, 2000), p. 180.

29 Malik, State and Civil Society in Pakistan, p. 95.

30 B. Raman, "Pakistan's Inter Service Intelligence (ISI)," SAAG paper no. 287, South Asia Analysis Group, January 8, 2001, <www.southasiaanalysis. org/%5Cpapers 3%5 Cpaper 287.html>.

31 Rizvi, "Civil-Military Relations in Contemporary Pakistan," p. 100.

32 Tim McGirk, "Has Pakistan Tamed Its Spies?" *Time*, May 6, 2002.

33   Hassan Abbas, Pakistan's Drift into Extremism: Allah, the Army, and America's War on Terror (Armonk, N.Y.: M. E. Sharpe, 2005), pp. 217–20.

34   *Daily Times*, October 8, 2002.

35   *Daily Times*, January 28, 2003.

36   Mushahid Hussain, "Reforming Intelligence," *Nation*, December 24, 2002.

37   *News*, June 26, 2007.

38   Shafqat Mahmood, "Covert Operations Fall Out," *News*, March 14, 2003.

39   Ibid.

40   Aziz-ud-Din Ahmad, "Dismantling Political Parties," *Nation*, October 2, 2003.

41   *Daily Times*, May 19, 2003.

42   *Nation*, March 14, 2003

43   Moreover, the fact that the leadership abdicated what should have been essentially its task is an interesting indicator of the degree of subordination of the ruling political class to the military establishment.

44   *South Asia Tribune*, December 30, 2002.

45   Francoise Chipaux, "Au Pakistan, l'armee a perdu toute credibilite aux yeux de l'opinion" [In Pakistan, the army has lost its credibility in the eyes of the public], *Le Monde*, November 10, 2007.

46   See Rizvi, "Civil-Military Relations in Contemporary Pakistan," p. 101.

47   *Muslim*, February 25, 1997.

48   Altaf Gauhar, "The Mysteries of Secret Service Funds," *Nation*, May 6, 1994.

49   *Muslim*, February 25, 1997.

50   *Pakistan Times*, June 17, 1997.

51   Malik, State and Civil Society in Pakistan, p. 293–40.

52 Muslim, February 25, 1997.

53 *Dawn*, February 5, 2007.

54 Seyyed Vali Reza Nasr, "Democracy and the Crisis of Governability in Pakistan," *Asian Survey*, vol. 32, no. 6 (June 1992), p. 523.

55 Rizvi, "Civil-Military Relations in Contemporary Pakistan," p. 101.

56 Malik, State and Civil Society in Pakistan, p. 98.

57 *Nation*, August 16, 2007.

58 See Rizvi, "Civil-Military Relations in Contemporary Pakistan," p. 101.

59 See for example, "JUI-F, JI, Accuse Secret Agencies for MMA Rift," *Dawn*, September 30, 2003.

60 Malik, State and Civil Society in Pakistan, p. 96.

61 Khalid Hasan, "Pakistan Intelligence Monster," *Daily Times*, January 14, 2007.

62 Hussain, "Reforming Intelligence."

63 Ibid.

64 The movement was later renamed Tehriq-e-Jafria Pakistan (TJP).

65 Mariam Abou Zahab, "The Regional Dimension of Sectarian Conflicts," in Christophe Jaffrelot, ed., Pakistan: Nationalism Without a Nation? (New Delhi: Manohar Publishers, 2002), p. 116.

66 Abbas, Pakistan's Drift into Extremism, p. 205.

67 Frédéric Grare, "The Evolution of Sectarian Conflicts in Pakistan and the Ever-Changing Face of Islamic Violence," *Journal of South Asian Studies*, vol. 30, no. 1 (April 2007), p. 130.

68 Seyyed Vali Reza Nasr, "Islam, the State and the Rise of Sectarian Militancy in Pakistan," in Christophe Jaffrelot, ed., Pakistan: Nationalism Without a Nation?

(New Delhi: Manohar Publishers, 2002), p. 87.

69  Nasr, "Islam, the State and the Rise of Sectarian Militancy," p. 92.

70  Abbas, Pakistan's Drift into Extremism, p. 205.

71  Ibid., p. 206.

72  Sohail Mahmood, Islamic Fundamentalism in Pakistan, Egypt and Iran (Lahore: Vanguard, 1995), p. 260.

73  Musa Khan Jalalzai, Sectarian Violence in Pakistan and Afghanistan (Lahore: System Books, 1999), p. 47.

74  Jhangvi was assassinated in 1990.

75  See "In the Spotlight: Lashkar-I-Jhangvi," Center for Defense Information, March 3, 2003, <www.cdi.org/terrorism/lij.cfm>.

76  Abbas, Pakistan's Drift into Extremism, p. 209.

77  Ibid.

78  Seyyed Vali Reza Nasr, "Regional Implications of Shia Revival in Iraq," *Washington Quarterly*, vol. 27, no. 3 (Summer 2004), p. 12.

79  Anwar Syed, "Role of the Intelligence Agencies," *Dawn*, July 30, 2006.

80  Malik, State and Civil Society in Pakistan, p. 230.

81  Ibid.

82  Syed, "Role of the Intelligence Agencies."

83  Abbas, Pakistan's Drift into Extremism, p. 147.

84  Ibid., p. 156.

85  "Pakistan: Emergency Rule or Return to Democracy, Crisis Alert," International Crisis Group, Islamabad/Washington/Brussels, June 6, 2007.

86  Farooq Hassan, "Constitutional Control of Intelligence Agencies in Pakistan" (background paper, Carnegie Endowment for International Peace, Washington, D.C., February 2008). Farooq Hassan is senior advocate, Supreme Court of Pakistan.

87  Ibid.

88  Ibid.

89  Ibid.

90  See State of Human Rights in 2007 (Lahore: Human Rights Commission of Pakistan, March 2008), pp. 76–78.

91  Najam U Din, "Terrorist Unless Proven Otherwise: Human Rights Implications of Anti-Terror Laws and Practices in Pakistan" (Lahore: Human Rights Commission of Pakistan, 2007), pp. 33–34.

92  Constitution of Pakistan, Art. 10(1), 1973.

93  Hassan, "Constitutional Control of Intelligence Agencies in Pakistan."

94  *News*, August 10, 2006.

95  *News*, October 8, 2006. The then federal interior minister Sherpao is said to have declared on December 19, 2005, that 4,000 people from Balochistan had been arrested; *News*, October 9, 2006.

96  *Post*, October 10, 2006.

97  *News*, November 9, 2006.

98  *Post*, April 30, 2007.

99  *Nation*, June 7, 2007.

100 *Dawn*, August 21, 2007.

101 *Dawn*, October 6, 2007.

102 *Dawn*, October 12, 2007.

103 The text had been drafted before the state of emergency was proclaimed.

104 *Nation*, November 11, 2007.

105 *Post*, December 20, 2007.

106 Because Benazir had already been dismissed, this could only mean President Ghulam Ishaq Khan.

107 Brigadier (ret.) A. R. Siddiqi, "ISI: The Political Dimension," *Nation*, July 30, 1997.

108 Gauhar, "The Mysteries of Secret Service Funds."

109 *Dawn,* July 12, 2006.

110 Siddiqi, "ISI: The Political Dimension," *Nation,* July 30, 1997.

111 *Daily Times,* September 14, 2002.

112 This does not exclude the possibility that rogue individuals may exist within the ISI as within any organization anywhere in the world.

113 Brigadier Syed A. I. Tirmazi, Profiles of Intelligence (Lahore: Intikhab-e-Jadeed Press, 1995), p. 422.

114 Malik, State and Civil Society in Pakistan, p. 98.

115 Winchell, "Pakistan's ISI: The Invisible Government," p. 381.

116 Ibid.

117 Raman, "Pakistan's Inter Service Intelligence (ISI)."

118 See Ian Talbot, Pakistan: A Modern History, (London: Hurst & Company, 1998), p. 309.

119 Ibid.

120 Malik, State and Civil Society in Pakistan, p. 100.

121 Ibid.

122 Winchell, "Pakistan's ISI: The Invisible Government," p. 381.

123 Raman, "Pakistan's Inter Service Intelligence (ISI)."

124 Rizvi, "Civil-Military Relations in Contemporary Pakistan," p. 101.

125 Abbas, Pakistan's Drift into Extremism, p. 186.

126 Abdul Sattar Khan, "Jamali's Eyes and Ears," *News,* December 3, 2002.

127 See "Reining in the Agencies," *Nation,* April 29, 2007.

128 Ibid. It should be observed, however, that on this occasion the two main agencies, MI and ISI, behaved

differently. The director general of MI followed Musharraf in his attempt to have the chief justice dismissed. The director general of the ISI, General Parvez Kayani, who has been appointed vice chief of army staff, did not. Farrukh Khan Pitafi, "Rethinking National Intelligence," Intelligence Review, 2007.

129 See "Proclamation of Emergency," Agence France-Presse, November 3, 2007.

130 Tariq Butt, "Agencies Ruling the Roost Since October 1999," *News*, June 2007.

131 *Dawn*, April 29, 2007.

132 Ibid.

133 "Charter of Democracy," May 2006.

134 "Towards Peace and Prosperity in Pakistan," Pakistan People's Party Manifesto, 2008, p. 16.

135 The date was postponed several times before the elections finally took place on February 18, 2008.

136 *Daily Times*, September 1, 2007.

137 *News*, October 27, 2007.

138 *Dawn,* October 27, 2007.

139 *Post*, October 29, 2007.

140 *Daily Times*, January 4, 2008.

141 *News*, February 13, 2008.

142 *Post*, May 10, 2008.

143 *News*, May 31, 2008.

144 *News*, April 23, 2008.

145 M. Ilyas Khan, "Spy Agency Confusion in Pakistan," BBC News, Karachi, July 28, 2008, <http://news.bbc.co.uk/2/hi/south_asia/7528592.stm>.

146 *News International*, July 28, 2008.

147 Omar Waraich, "Pakistan's Spies Elude Its Government," Time, July 31, 2008, <www.time/printout/0, 8816, 1828207, 00.html>.

148 *Australian*, July 28, 2008.

149 "Indonesia: Keeping the Military Under Control," ICG Asia Report no. 9, International Crisis Group, Jakarta/ Brussels, September 2000, pp. 12–13.

150 Damien Kingsbury, Power Politics and the Indonesian Military (New York: RoutledgeCurzon, 2003), p. 7.

151 Ibid.

152 Ibid.

153 Jun Honna, "Military Ideology in Response to Democratic Pressure During the Late Suharto Era: Political and Institutional Contexts," in Benedict R. O'G. Anderson, ed., Violence and the State in Suharto's Indonesia (Ithaca: Southeast Asia Program Publications, Southeast Asia Program, Cornell University, 2001), p. 55.

154 Ibid.

155 See Kingsbury, Power Politics and the Indonesian Military, p. 125.

156 Richard Tanter, "The Totalitarian Ambition: Intelligence Organisations in the Indonesian State," in Arief Budiman, ed., State and Civil Society in Indonesia (Clayton, Victoria, Australia: Centre of Southeast Asian Studies, Monash University, 1990), p. 221.

157 For a detailed description of the organization, see ibid., p. 223.

158 Ibid., p. 224.

159 Kingsbury, Power Politics and the Indonesian Military, p. 60.

160 See Tanter, "The Totalitarian Ambition," p. 229.

161 Between 500,000 and 750,000 people were arrested.

162 See Rabasa and Haseman, eds., The Military and Democracy in Indonesia, pp. 31, 34.

163 The bupati (district head) is also in charge of collecting taxes and receives funds from the central government.

164 See "Indonesia: Keeping the Military Under Control," p. 13.

165 Richard Tanter, "The Indonesian Intelligence State: Characteristics and Prospects" (paper prepared for the Australian Asian Studies Conference, University of Melbourne, July 2–5, 2000).

166 Siddarth Chandra and Douglas Kammen, "Generating Reforms and Reforming Generations: Military Politics in Indonesia's Democratic Transition and Consolidation," *World Politics*, vol. 55, no. 1 (October 2002), p. 101.

167 "Indonesia: Keeping the Military Under Control," p. 5.

168 Kingsbury, Power Politics and the Indonesian Military, p. 173.

169 Marcus Mietzner, The Politics of Military Reform in Post-Suharto Indonesia: Elite Conflict, Nationalism, and Institutional Resistance (Washington D.C.: East-West Center, 2006), p. 7.

170 "Indonesia: Keeping the Military Under Control," pp. 4–5.

171 For a detailed discussion see Kingsbury, Power Politics and the Indonesian Military, p. 173.

172 Tanter, "The Indonesian Intelligence State."

173 See "Indonesia: Keeping the Military Under Control," p. 7.

174 "Government Abolishes Bakorstanas, Litsus System," *Jakarta Post*, March 8, 2000

175 Ibid.

176 Mietzner, The Politics of Military Reform in Post-Suharto Indonesia, p. 60.

177 Tanter, "The Indonesian Intelligence State."

178 Ibid.

179 For a detailed description of the organizational changes of BAIS, see John Haseman, "Indonesia's New Look Intelligence Community," Jane's Intelligence Review, May 2000, pp. 28–29.

180 "Indonesia: Rethinking Internal Security Strategy," Asia Report no. 90, International Crisis Group, Jakarta/ Brussels, December 2004, p. 13.

181 Kingsbury, Power Politics and the Indonesian Military, p. 132.

182 Rabasa and Haseman, eds., The Military and Democracy in Indonesia, p. 31.

183 John Haseman, "Indonesia's Changing Role in the War on Terrorism," Jane's Intelligence Review, November 2002, p. 47.

184 Ibid., p. 14.

185 "Indonesia: Draft Intelligence Law Threatens Basic Rights," Human Rights Watch, August 2, 2005, <http:/ /hrw.org/english/docs/2005/08/03/ indone11548.htm>.

186 Kelly McEvers, "Indonesia's Expanding Spy Network Alarms Reformers," Christian Science Monitor, February 4, 2004.

187 "Indonesia: Rethinking Internal Security Strategy," p. 15.

188 John Haseman, "Indonesia's New Look Intelligence Community," p. 29.

189 Tanter, "The Totalitarian Ambition," p. 264.

190 Kingsbury, Power Politics and the Indonesian Military, p. 127.

191 Fabio Scarpello, "Indonesian Intelligence Service's Day in Court May Lead to Reform of Agency," World Politics Review, August 29, 2007. U.S. military assistance to Indonesia was, however, resumed in November 2005.

192 Ibid.

193 See also Samantha Brown, "Dossier Links Indonesian Intelligence to Activist Murder," Agence France-Presse, August 15, 2007.

194 In the previous presidential election, 40 percent of the electorate had voted for Allende and 30 percent for the Christian Democratic Party.

195 Gregory Weeks, "A Preference for Deference," p. 50.

196 J. Samuel Valenzuela and Arturo Valenzuela, eds., Military Rule in Chile: Dictatorship and Opposition (Baltimore: Johns Hopkins University Press, 1986), p. 131.

197 Gregory Weeks, "The Military and Intelligence Reform in Chile," Revista Fuerzas Armadas y Sociedad, vol. 18, no. 3–4, p. 260.

198 Valenzuela and Valenzuela, eds., Military Rule in Chile, p. 131.

199 Ibid., p. 132.

200 Claudio Heiss and Patricio Navia, "You Win Some, You Lose Some: Constitutional Reforms in Chile's Transition to Democracy," Latin American Politics and Society, vol. 49, no. 3 (Fall 2007), pp. 163–64.

201 Claudia A. Fuentes, "After Pinochet: Civilian Policies Toward the Military in the 1990s Chilean Democracy," Journal of Interamerican Studies and World Affairs, vol. 42, no. 3 (Autumn 2000), p. 120.

202 Ibid., p. 121.

203 Fuentes, "After Pinochet," p. 121.

204 Ibid., p. 127.

205 For a complete description of the jail episode, see Gregory Weeks, The Military and Politics in Postauthoritarian Chile (Tuscaloosa: University of Alabama Press, 2003), pp. 103–7.

206 Ibid., p. 113.

207 Pinochet's welcome as a national hero by the army and by his supporters upon his return to Chile proved much more controversial.

208 Weeks, The Military and Politics in Postauthoritarian Chile, p. 148.

209 See Nibaldo H. Galleguillos, "Studying Civil-Military Relations in the Post- Dictatorship Era: An Analysis of the Chilean Experience," *Journal of Third World Studies*, vol. 17, no. 2 (Fall 2000), p. 99.

210 Quoted in Heiss and Navia, "You Win Some, You Lose Some," p. 184.

211 Management of Public Security and Information, Law 19.212, Art. 2.

212 Ibid., Art. 3.

213 Ibid., Title II, Art. 5.

214 Weeks, "The Military and Intelligence Reform in Chile," p. 259.

215 Weeks, "A Preference for Deference," p. 52.

216 Ibid.

217 About the Intelligence System and the Creation of the National Intelligence Agency, Law 19.974, Art. 7-a.

218 Gregory Weeks, "A Preference for Deference: Reforming the Military's Intelligence Role in Argentina, Chile and Peru," p. 52–53.

219 About the Intelligence System and the Creation of the National Intelligence Agency, Art. 9.

220 Gregory Weeks, "A Preference for Deference," p. 52–53.

221 Felipe Agüero, "The New 'Double Challenge': Simultaneously Crafting Democratic Control and Efficacy Concerning Military, Police and Intelligence" (working document prepared for the third general assembly of the Club of Madrid, November 12–13, 2004).

222 "Reforming Pakistan's Police," Asia Report no. 157, International Crisis Group, Brussels, July 2008.

223 Ibid.

224 South Africa, where the intelligence agencies were restructured after the end of apartheid, initiated a similar process and redefined the goals of the Government of National Unity in a comprehensive Reconstruction and Development Program. It then published a white paper on intelligence before defining the philosophy, mission, and role of intelligence in a democratic South Africa within this framework; see "White Paper on Intelligence."

# INDEX